# COSTLY GRACE

# COSTLY GRACE

A Contemporary View of
**DIETRICH BONHOEFFER'S**
The Cost of Discipleship

## JON WALKER

LEAFWOOD
PUBLISHERS

# COSTLY GRACE
A Contemporary View of Dietrich Bonhoeffer's
The Cost of Discipleship

Copyright © 2010 Jon Walker

ISBN 978-0-89112-676-8
LCCN 2010034712

LIBRARY OF CONGRESS CATALOGING-IN-PUBLICATION DATA
Walker, Jon, 1958-
Costly grace : a contemporary view of Dietrich Bonhoeffer's The cost of discipleship / Jon Walker.
   p. cm.
ISBN 978-0-89112-676-8
1.  Bonhoeffer, Dietrich, 1906-1945. Nachfolge. 2.  Christian life. 3.  Grace (Theology) I. Title.
BT380.B6593 W35 2010
248.4--dc22

                                            2010034712

Cover and interior text design by Thinkpen Design, Inc.

Published in association with Rosenbaum & Associates Literary Agency, Brentwood, Tennessee.

Leafwood Publishers is an imprint of Abilene Christian University Press
1626 Campus Court
Abilene, Texas 79601

1-877-816-4455
www.leafwoodpublishers.com

              10 11 12 13 14 15 / 7 6 5 4 3 2 1

# DEDICATION

*To Grace Guthrie, who is the embodiment of grace,*
*and David and Susan Moffitt, whose generosity overwhelms me.*

# Acknowledgements

It is impossible to write a book without admitting, like Tennyson, "I am part of all that I have met." That being the case, it is beyond my abilities to thank everyone who helped me while writing this manuscript, but I do want to mention contributions by Steve Pettit, Mark Kelly, Lori Hensley, Matt Tullos, Tobin Perry, Paul Carlisle, Dan Stone, Susan Goetz, Denny Boultinghouse, and Rick Warren. My thanks also to Kathy Chapman Sharp, Donna Stetzer, Doug Hart, Bucky Rosenbaum, Gary Myers, Leonard Allen, Terry Whaley, Jordan Camenker, Kim Glaner, Sam Butler, Jason Elkins, David Chrzan, Robert Supernor, Ryan Carson, Kristine Noelle, Sally Killian, Christopher Walker, Nathan Walker, and Laura Vest, whose gift of Pumpkin the cockapoo quite honestly saved my life.

# CONTENTS

# FOREWORD

Contrary to popular book titles, there are no *Easy Steps to Christian Maturity* or *Secrets of Instant Sainthood*. Mature Christians are grown through struggles and storms and seasons of suffering. But most of all they are grown through obedience to Jesus.

*The Cost of Discipleship* helped me understand this when I read Dietrich Bonhoeffer's book as a young believer. In fact, it is one of the reasons I've spent a lifetime encouraging believers to follow Jesus with purpose, to surrender their lives wholeheartedly to him.

Sadly, millions of Christians are confused about what it means to surrender to Jesus and so they go on living their lives without ever changing the way they live. The "cheap grace" that Bonhoeffer describes in *The Cost of Discipleship* has so deeply saturated our congregations that, despite our evangelical theology, the idea of surrender is as unpopular and misunderstood as the idea of submission.

Surrender implies losing, and no one wants to be a loser. Yet, Jesus says we must be losers, losing our lives in order to find life in him (Matthew 16:25-28).

We speak too often of winning, succeeding, overcoming, and conquering and too little of yielding, submitting, obeying, and surrendering. Yet, we can only follow Jesus when we obey Jesus and his commands. To say "No, Lord" is to speak a contradiction.

Surrendered people obey God's word, even if it doesn't make sense. Surrendered hearts show up best in relationships. You don't edge others out, you don't demand your rights, and you aren't self-serving when you're surrendered. Being surrendered to Jesus costs us just as it cost Jesus when he surrendered himself to the cross for us.

*Costly Grace* by my friend and associate, Jon Walker, teaches that God will do his deepest work in you when you surrender to God and become obedient to the commands of Jesus (James 4:7). Instead of trying harder to be a Christian, you must trust Jesus more. Nothing under his control can ever be out of control. Mastered by Christ, you can handle anything.

The book *Costly Grace* is about the *practice of surrender*, which is a moment-by-moment, lifelong obedience to Jesus. We cannot call ourselves disciples of Jesus without this daily obedience to him: "And he said to them all, 'If you want to come with me, you must forget yourself, take up your cross every day, and follow me'" (Luke 9:23).

My prayer is that this book will remind the evangelical community that our lives not only can be changed when we follow Jesus, they *must* change or we have to question if we're really following Jesus. I believe *Costly Grace* may be one of the most important books published during this time of economic uncertainty and world turmoil. It strips discipleship down to its essentials, where we discover again that, when we face uncertainty, our only certainty is in Jesus.

Rick Warren

AUTHOR OF *The Purpose Driven Life*

# DIETRICH BONHOEFFER

Dietrich Bonheoffer's life was one of risk, where he faced constant choices that required him to take a stand, often putting everything he had—even his life—on the line for what he believed. It's easy to marvel at the way he faced off against Adolf Hitler and the Nazi regime, but in books such as "The Cost of Discipleship" Bonhoeffer teaches that a life of such extraordinary risk is the *expectation*, not the exception, for any disciple of Jesus.

To me, what is appealing about the Bonhoeffer is his authenticity. He walked steadily toward an uncompromising faith in Jesus and he did it in the difficult and dangerous reality of life, where obeying the commands of Christ can often be heart-wrenching and costly. Perhaps because he was thrust so quickly and so young into life or death matters, Bonhoeffer did not play games with pastoral piety or write from an ivory tower.

Too young to be ordained when he first graduated from seminary, Bonhoeffer continued his theological studies at Union Theological Seminary in New York City, and for a brief time taught Sunday school at Abyssinian Baptist Church in Harlem, New York. There Adam Clayton Powell Sr. preached a social gospel that would significantly influence the Civil Rights movement in the United States.

It was Powell who first used the term "cheap grace" to describe the way the church compromises the gospel when it down-plays the cross and repentance in order to sell an easy discipleship that requires little commitment and suggests there is a pain-free path into heaven. The take-away for Bonhoeffer was that, to echo his own words, his religious phraseology quickly transformed into real Christian action. For such a time as this, God sent him back to Germany.

It was a little over a year after Bonhoeffer was ordained as a Lutheran pastor that the Nazi's came to power on January 30, 1933. Bonhoeffer, still only twenty-six-years-old, delivered a radio address two days later, where he warned the German people they were being seduced by the Führer and that their worship of him would lead to idolatry. His broadcast was cut off in mid-sentence.

The young pastor watched in dismay as the state-sponsored church of Germany compromised with Hitler and so he became a founding member of the Confessing Church, which was comprised of congregations independent of government sponsorship. A gifted theologian, Bonhoeffer might have taught in any number of professorships or pastorates, but his opposition to Adolf Hitler closed the door to those opportunities. Instead, he began teaching in less formal settings, such as the unofficial Finkenwalde Seminary.

It was at Finkenwalde that Bonhoeffer began writing "The Cost of Discipleship," publishing the manuscript in 1937, about the same time the Gestapo shut down the seminary and arrested many of its students.

In 1939 Bonhoeffer returned to Union Theological Seminary in New York City to teach, but almost immediately regretted his decision, believing he would have no right to participate in the reconstruction of Christian life in Germany after the war if he wasn't there to share in the hardships of the German people during the war.

Returning to Germany, Bonhoeffer joined the *Abwehr*, a branch of Germany's military intelligence, but also the center for the resistance movement in Germany. For instance, the *Abwehr* worked to undermine Nazi policy toward the Jews and Bonhoeffer, in the sense of a double agent, used his position as cover to travel freely and speak to other believers, something he would not otherwise be allowed to do.

Although Bonhoeffer was a pacifist, he struggled with the moral obligations a believer faces when confronted with a systemic evil that saturates an entire society and, in this sense, he began fighting for the moral survival of the German people by opposing the Nazi regime. Bonhoeffer was not only aware of various plots against Hitler, he eventually saw the Führer's assassination as a necessity part of restoring the soul of Germany.

His arrest in April 1943 was not for involvement in these plots, but because the Gestapo suspected him of using the *Abwehr* as a way to cover Bonhoeffer's continuing work with the Confessing Church. While awaiting trail, Bonhoeffer continued his ministry from prison, secretly writing material that was eventually published posthumously as *Letters and Papers from Prison*.

After the July 20 plot ("Valkyrie") to assassinate Hitler failed, the Gestapo discovered Bonhoeffer's involvement and his death was ordered by Adolf Hitler.

Bonhoeffer was executed on April 8, 1945 by hanging at Flossenbürg concentra-
tion camp—about three weeks before Hitler committed suicide and the Allies
pushed into Berlin.

Bonhoeffer died as he lived, focused exclusively on Christ and humbly submitting to the ultimate cost of discipleship. Offered an opportunity to escape, he
declined, not wanting to put his family in danger. He was led to the gallows
after concluding a Sunday morning service, saying: "This is the end—for me the
beginning of life."[1]

He has become one of the most influential theological voices of the twentieth
century and *The Cost of Discipleship* is considered a classic in ecclesiological
literature. Many of its concepts are now deeply ingrained in modern Protestant
thought and practice.

If you'd like to read more about Bonhoeffer, see the excellent biography by
Eric Metaxas, *Bonhoeffer: Pastor, Martyr, Prophet, Spy* (Thomas Nelson, 2010).

INTRODUCTION

# CHRIST AND CHRIST ALONE

*"So what do we do? Keep on sinning so God can keep on forgiving? I should
hope not! If we've left the country where sin is sovereign, how can we still
live in our old house there? Or didn't you realize we packed up and left
there for good? That is what happened in baptism. When we went under
the water, we left the old country of sin behind; when we came up out of the
water, we entered into the new country of grace—a new life in a new land!"*

ROMANS 6:1-3 (MSG)

Most of us would like to live a life of extraordinary quality that is not only
fulfilling but also carries significance beyond ourselves. That's most
likely one of the reasons you became a Christian, and it is *exactly* the kind of life
Jesus promises if we will follow him.

So why isn't it happening? Why, instead of the abundant life, do so many of
us end up living lives of *quiet desperation*? We go to church; we read the Bible; we
pray; we try to be good people and to serve other people; yet, for many of us, our
life with Jesus doesn't seem to be much more than an add-on to our increasingly
complex lives, where we are over-stretched and now seem to be facing a tsunami
of uncertainty in many areas that for so long have seemed relatively secure—
our finances, our jobs, our homes, and even our fundamental safety.

So we try harder, work harder, pray harder, study harder, and try to figure out
what we're doing wrong because that's what we think Jesus wants us to do. And,
all the while, he keeps asking, in a sense, *"Are you tired of this yet?" "Worn out?
Burned out on religion? Come to me. Get away with me and you'll recover your life. I'll
show you how to take a real rest. Walk with me and work with me—watch how I do it.
Learn the unforced rhythms of grace"* (Matthew 11:28b-29 MSG).

Jesus calls us away from the hows and whys and whats into the rhythms of his
grace, standing before us as the Son of God Incarnate, Jesus, God's Word in the
flesh. The answer to our frustrations is "who," not "what" or "how."

The Word of God who stands before us is not a problem to be solved, but a person to know; when we try to relate to him as a "how" or "what," we end up in the never-ending cycle of trying harder to fit into an equation that God never meant for us to solve.

Instead of trying harder, we need to trust more.

None of this is new, and the danger as you read this is that you may dismiss it as so much religious lingo. "I know it is a relationship; I know I need to trust him."

Yet, we slip right back into the cycle of trying harder and that means the extraordinary life we want to live is diminished and defeated. My hope is that, in reading this book, you'll be able to step into the rhythm of grace Jesus died to provide and that you won't just stand there, but that you'll dance with the eternal Lover of your soul.

God's gift of grace, the Incarnation of Jesus—those are supernatural mysteries delivered by the God who always was and always will be; but walking in that grace isn't so much a mystery that we can only hope to get there someday. Jesus died and was resurrected so you could get there today and stay there every day of your life. You can access it at any time.

## JESUS DOESN'T KEEP YOU GUESSING

Jesus is not like some sneaky teacher who leaves you guessing about what you'll be graded on or who throws in trick questions on a test that require you to read obscure footnotes. He wants you to succeed and that's why the gospel is plain and simple, and the life of Christ Jesus is so easy to access.

We're the ones who complicate it by making discipleship—the practice of following Jesus—either unnecessarily difficult or needlessly confusing. Worse, we've reduced it to a series of religious exercises, such as book studies, Sunday school lessons, small group material, or intensive church-wide campaigns, when the objective, so often and easily lost, is for us to know Jesus at a level of intimacy that can only be sustained by his constant presence in our lives.

We tend to approach God's Word as simply a dispenser of facts and we wonder why our knowledge seems like hollow wisdom. Jesus even addressed this concern, saying, *"You search the Scriptures because you believe they give you eternal life. But the Scriptures point to me! Yet you refuse to come to me so that I can give you this eternal life"* (John 5:39–40 NLT).

Bonhoeffer's concern when he wrote *The Cost of Discipleship* was that the church had lost its focus on Jesus and, therefore, had lost the meaning of discipleship. Discipleship means we are inseparably bonded to Jesus. Without him, there can be no discipleship: he is the curriculum we study; he is the Word we believe; and he is the Way we live. *"Keep company with me and you'll learn to live freely and lightly,"* Jesus says (Matthew 11:30 MSG).

Jesus is our textbook on how to live connected to God, how to make decisions with the mind of Christ, and how to act on promptings from the Spirit rather than self-impulse. The more intimate we become with Jesus, the more successful we will be at becoming like him.

This is why we're to preach and teach Christ and Christ alone.

Bonheoffer saw the church abandoning Christ in two ways and both are as prevalent today as they were in Bonheoffer's generation.

*First, Bonhoeffer says the church has reduced the gospel to a set of burdensome rules*, the antithesis of the easy yoke we should find in Jesus. We've loaded the gospel down with so many extra-biblical routines and regulations—a *real Christian ought to, has to, must do*—that it is difficult for anyone to find the real Jesus, let alone make a clear and conscious decision to follow Christ.

We proclaim a religion of rules, which appeals to our prideful desire to show God we're good enough for his kingdom. We make our legal lists and that makes us legalists. Essentially, we're teaching people they have to work their way up to God's standard of righteousness, which challenges the very Word of God, who is the crucified and resurrected Jesus. It is a hopeless proposition and God meant it to be so—he wants us to understand that we can't because only Jesus can.

When we keep insisting that, through our behaviors and our attitudes, we can match godly standards of righteousness, is it any wonder why the world sees Jesus as insignificant?

*Second, Bonhoeffer says we've wrapped the gospel in a sense of false hopes*, using the doctrine of grace as an excuse for shallow discipleship and a pervasive acceptance of sin in the Body of Christ. Grace is meant to justify the sinner; yet, we use it to justify our sins. In other words, we've taken "I am a sinner saved by grace" and turned it into "I can sin because of grace." Because of this, we've become satisfied with discipleship as mere Bible study, maybe a weekly prayer breakfast, and for the really committed, a handful of rules to follow that make us feel and look particularly pious.

In either case—a burdensome religion or a presumptive attitude on grace—we end up practicing a religion far removed from the intimate relationship God wants us to have with Jesus Christ.

## JESUS BRINGS US GRACE AND TRUTH

On the surface, both these extremes look a bit like following Jesus, but my friend and long-time spiritual mentor Steve Pettit says they both attempt to do the impossible: the first tries to separate grace from truth and the second tries to separate truth from grace—either way, it only creates a monumental mess where, instead of becoming monuments to God's grace, we become monuments to our own foolish pride.

The apostle John tells us that Jesus is full of grace and truth and, now that we have the life of Christ present in our lives, we are full of grace and truth (John 1:14-16). Jesus holds them together in us just as they are held together in him.

Pettit says legalists like to dismiss grace while those unrestrained by grace (licentious) want to disregard truth. "Both groups end up paddling around in the seas of life with one oar in the water wondering why they keep going around in circles," says Pettit. "Both try to soar in the rarified air of the heavenlies, but with only one wing, and then they wonder why they can't get off the ground."

Since Jesus embodies the unity of God's Word (truth) and God's activity (grace), we're quickly greeted by the spirit of error when we try to process either grace or truth apart from the person of Jesus Christ. On the one hand, when we seek life and freedom by following the rules (laws, principles, truths separate from grace), we easily slip into legalism. How do we know when this has happened? Says Pettit, "Grace will be seen as license; it will sound like heresy." On the other hand, when we seek life and freedom in self-determination, in choosing whatever feels or seems good, when we become unrestrained by grace (licentious), Pettit says truth will be seen as "law." Truth sounds like legalism if we are abusing grace.

We're meant to seek life and freedom only in Jesus Christ. The fullness of both grace and truth are in him. "His grace is always truthful; his truth is forever gracious," says Pettit. "There is no way to have the fullness of grace and truth apart from him. He didn't come to show us ways of grace and truth or give us definitions of grace and truth. He came to be all the grace and all the truth we will ever need and to freely offer *both* to us in the gift of himself."

If I am full of grace, there is no excuse for legalism in my life (Matthew 23:4; 11:28-30).

If I am full of truth, there is no excuse for unrestraint (licentiousness) either (Matthew 5:17-20; John 8:11).

The only reason to live legalistically or licentiously is unbelief in the adequacy of the indwelling Lord Jesus Christ who freely supplies grace and truth for my every need. Or an unwillingness to let him be himself—full of a grace and truth—in and through me.

We must go to Jesus, not only to learn how to live, but to receive the life from which we live—his life placed in us to create in us the righteousness of God and the characteristics of Christ. The essence of discipleship, then, is to know Jesus at a level of intimacy that can only be sustained by his constant presence in our lives.

As we follow Jesus, we find he consistently moves us toward a choice—and then he commands us to make the choice: Will you believe I am adequate to meet your needs or not? Will you let me be myself in and through you or not? In a sense, he often frames the choice as: Will you follow me into the kingdom of heaven, or will you remain a citizen of this world? Will you set your mind on things above or keep it on earthly things? (Colossians 3:2)

The kingdom of heaven can be entered into now and we are meant to live there *in the now*. It is not a kingdom in a far and distant future. When we follow Jesus, we follow him into the kingdom and there we learn to live according to the rules and laws established by our King. We live as citizens of that world and not this world.

## FOLLOWING AFTER JESUS

You can remain in the kingdom of this world, but if you do, Bonhoeffer notes, you are not a disciple of Jesus. (In German, the title for Bonhoeffer's book is *Nachfolge*, essentially "discipleship," but quite literally "following after." We follow after Jesus.) Bonhoeffer argues that when we live as a citizen of this world, we seek easy choices that lead to an easy life. However, when Jesus brings us to a choice, the choice itself is easy, it is our decision that is hard because to follow Jesus means to abandon the life of apparent convenience.

But if we follow Jesus, he "asks nothing of us without giving us the strength to perform it," says Bonhoeffer. "His commandment never seeks to destroy life, but to foster, strengthen, and heal it." *"And his commands are not too hard for us,"* says the apostle John (1 John 5:3). Bonhoeffer says the commands of Jesus allow us to "escape from the hard yoke" of our own religious traditions.

Jesus is not arbitrary or naive in his rule. He knows the realities of this life but he also knows the realities of eternity. His eye is on the endgame. He knows there will be a judgment for those outside his grace and so he approaches this world with a different point of view. Even on the cross, his prayer was for forgiveness and not vengeance and that is a perspective we learn as we move from thinking like fallen beings to thinking like citizens of the kingdom of heaven (Do we engage in fallen thinking or kingdom thinking?)

We may not understand all Jesus does and that scares us, but that is also where faith emerges. It is at this critical junction between fear and faith that we can see the cost of discipleship clearly, and so Jesus pushes us constantly to this place of choice, where we follow in faith or pull back in fear.

By retreating in fear, unwilling to pay the cost of discipleship, Bonhoeffer suggests we act as our own obstacles to Jesus and his Word. Do we follow dogma instead of Jesus? Do we create *impersonal* discipleship models that are hopelessly irrelevant to our *personal* lives? Do we preach, teach, and discuss the same biblical concepts over and over again—our favorite ones—at the expense of others that are just as important? Do we follow Jesus based more on our own opinions and convictions, and too little on the commands of Christ?

We must look to Jesus and no where else for our answers. We must know a Christ who is real and solid, and this knowing doesn't come from conveniently memorizing Bible facts or comfortably studying theological systems. It comes in the willingness to pay the cost of knowing him and sacrificially living out of what we believe to be true of him.

Jesus wants you to know him. He wants you to live an extraordinary life, full of grace and truth. He calls you to a miraculous life, one that requires edge-of-your-seat faith to follow him, where you find yourself asking in joy, "What's next, Jesus? What are you going to do though me today?"

You can have that. Jesus calls, you must respond. My prayer is that this book will help you see the simplicity of following Jesus while also helping you understand the cost of such discipleship.

Jon Walker
JACOB'S LANDING
AUGUST 2010

# 1

## GRACE AND DISCIPLESHIP

*What shall we say, then? Should we continue to live in sin so that God's grace will increase? Certainly not! We have died to sin—how then can we go on living in it?*

ROMANS 6:1-2

Dietrich Bonhoeffer declared cheap grace the deadly enemy of our church in 1937. "We are fighting today for costly grace," he said. We are in that same fight today.

By cheap grace, Bonhoeffer means the arrogant presumption that we can receive forgiveness for our sins, yet never abandon our lives to Jesus. We *assume*, since grace is free, there is no cost associated with the free gift. *We assume* we can go on living the way we have been because our sins are now forgiven.

The gift is free, but Jesus paid a bloody price to offer us the gift; the gift is free, but that doesn't mean there is no cost to following Jesus once we step into his grace.

Costly grace justifies the sinner: *Go and sin no more*. Cheap grace justifies the sin: *Everything is forgiven, so you can stay as you are*.

"Cheap grace is the preaching of forgiveness without requiring repentance, baptism without church discipline, Communion without confession, absolution without personal confession," says Bonhoeffer. "Cheap grace is grace without discipleship, grace without the cross, grace without Jesus Christ, living and incarnate."

And this means cheap grace is "a denial of the incarnation of the Word of God," says Bonhoeffer. Did Jesus die so we could follow a doctrine? Did he suffer a cruel and bloody crucifixion to give us a code of conduct? Did he give up all he had, take on the nature of a servant and walk through Palestine as a human being so we could give an intellectual assent to the grace he freely gives? Did he

25

humble himself and walk the path of obedience all the way to death so we could live in disobedience to him? (based on Philippians 2:8)

When the forgiveness of sin is proclaimed as a general truth and the love of God taught as an abstract concept, we depersonalize the incarnation; yet, it can't be anything but personal: the God of the universe launching a rescue mission for you, his beloved creation, at the expense of Jesus, his only begotten son. Jesus didn't come in the abstract, as a nebulous idea of love, grace, and forgiveness; rather, "he became like a human being and appeared in human likeness" (Philippians 2:7b).

You can't get more personal than that.

The Incarnation is totally personal. When Jesus calls you it is absolutely personal; and the cost of grace is personal. Jesus paid personally to provide us with free grace and we must pay personally to live within that grace. Why do you think Jesus died for you, if not for the personal? What do you think he expects from you, if not something personal?

## RATIONALIZING OUR WAY INTO CHEAP GRACE

We too easily slip into a corporate concept that Jesus died for sins *in general* and so he becomes to us something like a huge corporation: we don't really expect to get personal, individualized attention. And because everything, in our thinking, is impersonal, it is easier for us to dodge responsibility.

In the case of the cross, it is the difference between "Jesus died for the sins of mankind" or "Jesus died to pay for my lie last week at work."

This is how we rationalize our way into cheap grace. But we are called—in truth, we are designed— to come face-to-face with Jesus, which allows us get to know him and the Father as we are know by them: "What we see now is like a dim image in a mirror; then we shall see face-to-face. What I know now is only partial; then it will be complete—as complete as God's knowledge of me" (1 Corinthians 13:12).

On the one hand, costly grace cost Jesus his life and he gives it to us as a gift of righteousness that includes the forgiveness of sin; it is something we can never earn and it comes to us as we open our hearts in repentance: "Have mercy on me, O God, because of your unfailing love. Purify me from my sin. For I recognize my rebellion; it haunts me day and night. Against you, and you alone, have I sinned; I have done what is evil in your sight. Create in me a clean heart, O God. Renew a loyal spirit within me" (Psalms 51:1-4, 10 NLT).

On the other hand, Bonhoeffer says cheap grace requires no contrition; we need not even have a desire to be *delivered* from our sins, just forgiven. He says, "Cheap grace is the grace we bestow on ourselves." *It's okay, God will forgive me.*

"Costly grace is the treasure hidden in the field; for the sake of it a man will gladly go and sell all that he has," says Bonhoeffer. "It is the pearl of great price to buy which the merchant will sell all his goods. It is the kingly rule of Christ, for whose sake a man will pluck out the eye which causes him to stumble; it is the call of Jesus Christ at which the disciple leaves his nets and follows him."

Costly grace comes when we come to the end of ourselves, ready to abandon our current lives in order to give our lives whole-heartedly to Jesus. It comes when it is no longer I who live, but Christ who lives in me (Galatians 2:20). It comes when we submit ourselves to the will of Jesus, doing what he tells us to do day-in-and-day-out, *altering* our lives in obedience to him.

Costly grace means we change our habits, thoughts, behaviors, attitudes, and relationships according to the will of Jesus. Nothing can remain the same because we are no longer the same. We are uniquely connected to the divine nature through Jesus and we no longer "live under law but under God's grace" (Romans 6:14; see also Colossians 2:9-10).

"Such grace is costly because it calls us to follow, and it is grace because it calls us to follow Jesus Christ," says Bonhoeffer. "It is costly because it costs a man his life, and it is grace because it gives a man the only true life. It is costly because it condemns sin, and grace because it justifies the sinner."

## GRACE AND DISCIPLESHIP ARE INSEPARABLE

"When he spoke of grace, [Martin] Luther always implied as a corollary that it cost him his own life, the life which was now for the first time subjected to the absolute obedience of Christ," says Bonhoeffer. Costly grace does not exempt us from discipleship or give us a pass on obeying the commands of Jesus. In fact, it demands "we take the call to discipleship more seriously than ever before."

And grace doesn't make our sanctification automatic; Jesus transforms us into his image as we follow him down the hard path through the narrow gate into the kingdom of heaven. Luther quickly understood that discipleship must be tested in the world, outside the cloister, as Jesus pushes us from self-centered to other-centered.

While it is true Luther said, "Sin boldly, but believe and rejoice in Christ more boldly still," Bonhoeffer notes his intent was not to teach cheap grace but to help us understand our position in Christ. When we get serious about discipleship, we will want to be obedient to God. This is why Jesus said the way we show our love for him is by being obedient to his commands. Our obedience brings us in line with the will of God; we become one with his agenda. And that's the essence of love: when we love we want to do the things the people we love want to do; we become one with our loved one's wishes.

Yet, our obedience will never make us perfect. The only way we can approach the throne of grace boldly is by stepping into the costly grace of Christ, where he becomes our righteousness before God; he acts as our mediator. Luther's point, then, was when we sin we need not despair. Jesus covers all our sins. He died for the sins you've already committed and he died for the sins you will commit tomorrow. Luther means we can stop being afraid of ourselves; stop being afraid that we may make mistakes. Just love God and live your life—and when you stumble, fall into the grace of Jesus Christ.

By trusting the grace of God, we can be courageous in following Jesus and equally courageous in confessing our sins before him. There is no need to hide our sins or to posture as if we have not sinned. We can just admit it and keep on following Jesus, even if we have to confess sins to Jesus every day.

But if we don't have a clear understanding of costly grace, we're more likely to play games with God, pretending we haven't sinned, maintaining the delusion that we're not that bad, and that leaves us stuck in immaturity right at the threshold of discipleship. And our posturing is part of how we undermine grace. If we're so cheaply forgiven, then we never have to face the ugliness of our sin. It doesn't seem so bad. The bloody work and resurrection of Jesus become a generic work, a blanket forgiving of sins, a prettified passion meant to *God bless us, everyone*.

Cheap grace flips Luther's *sin without fear* upside-down, recreating it as a justification of sin instead of the justification of the sinner. Bonhoeffer says the real "outcome of the Reformation was the victory, not of Luther's perception of grace in all its purity and costliness, but of the vigilant religious instinct of man

for the place where grace is to be obtained at the cheapest price." "The justification of the sinner in the world degenerated into the justification of sin and
the world," Bonhoeffer says. "Costly grace was turned into cheap grace without discipleship."

This is exactly what Paul addresses with the church in Rome, where the *religious instinct of man*—that desire for self-justification—was in full assault against
the sovereignty of God, attempting to prove God wrong in his bloody sacrifice
of Jesus.

## DOES GRACE MEAN WE CAN KEEP ON SINNING?

*"So what do we do? Keep on sinning so God can keep on forgiving?" asks Paul. I should
hope not! If we've left the country where sin is sovereign, how can we still live in our old
house there? Or didn't you realize we packed up and left there for good? That is what happened in baptism. When we went under the water, we left the old country of sin behind;
when we came up out of the water, we entered into the new country of grace—a new life in
a new land! That's what baptism into the life of Jesus means"* (Romans 6:1-3 MSG).

The costly grace of Jesus means to take us into a new land, the kingdom of
heaven. We follow Jesus obediently along a difficult path through a narrow gate
into his kingdom.

A simple glance across the evangelical landscape reveals that we've overwhelmingly embraced the lesser grace. We're barely willing to adjust our schedules let
alone our lifestyles. We make decisions based on common sense, robbing the
Holy Spirit of his role of counsel. We stash away our 401k's and plan for when
we will do kingdom work in the future, never trusting God to provide. We take
the risk out of ministry by always leaning on our own understanding and then
we wonder why our faith is weak. When do we exercise our faith?

We're glad to follow Jesus. His yoke does seem easy: a few hours each week in
worship, a Bible study, a small group, a bit of service at the church and perhaps
a mission trip each year. We try to be good people, to help others, and to thank
God for our blessings. When things are going well, we don't want to bother God
and, when things are going badly, we can camp out with God and say a holy
"Amen" that he's always there in our darkest times.

But a peculiar people? A royal priesthood set apart? What? Does Jesus really
mean I'm supposed to abandon my _____ (fill in the blank)?

We preach, we teach, we publish. We have the internet and Christian radio. "We poured forth unending streams of grace," says Bonhoeffer. But the call to follow Jesus in the narrow way is hardly ever heard. Have we presented the gospel in such a way that we've left people feeling secure in their ungodly living?

Cheap grace has been "disastrous to our own spiritual lives," says Bonhoeffer. "Instead of opening up the way to Christ, it has closed it. Instead of calling us to follow Christ, it has hardened us in our disobedience."

We've settled for cheap grace for so long that we've allowed it to become the norm for Christian living. We know there must be something more but life just gets in the way. We've taught people to live disconnected from Jesus and we wonder why they struggle in their Christian walk, why they are so tired all the time.

Bonhoeffer says, "To put it quite simply, we must undertake this task because we are now ready to admit that we no longer stand in the path of true discipleship. We confess that, although our Church is orthodox as far as her doctrine of grace is concerned, we are no longer sure that we are members of a Church which follows its Lord. We must therefore attempt to recover a true understanding of the mutual relation between grace and discipleship. The issue can no longer be evaded. It is becoming clearer every day that the most urgent problem besetting our Church is this: How can we live the Christian life in the modern world?"

## THINK OF GRACE AS A RESTAURANT

Grace is a restaurant where you can eat anything on the menu for free. The cost for you to dine is hefty, but your whole bill has been paid by Jesus.

"You mean, I can eat anything I want here? Then I'll have a lust burger with a side of lies."

I'm sorry. We don't serve lust burgers or lies here. But you are welcome to anything on the menu. Everything here is hand-made by the Father and all of it is specifically designed to keep you healthy.

"I thought you said I could eat anything I wanted if I came into this grace restaurant?"

You can eat anything you want, but we only serve what is on the menu. If you look, you will see there are thousands of choices we've prepared specifically for your taste buds.

"But not a lust burger? No lie fries. What kind of restaurant are you running here? Don't you want me to be happy, to feel good?"

Happy are those whose greatest desire is to do what God requires; God will satisfy them fully!

"What if I go outside the restaurant, get a lust burger and some lie fries, and bring them back in here to eat?"

That would be cheap grace.

## GRACE IS A TRANSFORMING POWER

If you asked most evangelical Christians about the meaning of grace, they'd probably tell you it's the unmerited favor of God. Not a bad answer, but one that's just academic enough to keep you distracted from the truly transformational nature of costly grace.

Grace is powerful, audacious, and dangerous, and if it ever got free reign in our churches, it would begin a transformation so rapid and radical that it would cause skeptics to beat a path to our door.

What is grace? Consider this illustration from *Les Miserables*, Victor Hugo's timeless tale about a peasant who is sentenced to hard labor for stealing a loaf of bread. Released from jail, Jean Valjean is offered brief sanctuary in the home of a priest.

Despite being treated with dignity for the first time in years, Valjean, steals the bishop's valuable silverware and runs away. The next day, Valjean is brought back to the priest's home by the police, who tell the priest that Valjean has claimed the silver as a gift. The police obviously expect the priest to deny the claim.

The priest immediately addresses Valjean, saying, "Ah, there you are! I am glad to see you. But I gave you the candlesticks also, which are silver like the rest, and would bring two hundred francs. Why did you not take them along with your plates?" When he hands the candlesticks to Valjean privately, he tells him, "Jean Valjean, my brother, you belong no longer to evil, but to good. It is your soul that I am buying for you."

It's a Christ-like moment—and one that shows the tremendous cost of grace, both for the giver and the receiver. Valjean goes on to live a life of grace, supporting the poor and adopting a young orphan whom he must ransom out of servitude.

Do you suppose for a minute that a harsher approach by the priest could have gotten a better response from Jean Valjean? Then why do we expect people to behave better when we "Tsk, tsk, tsk" and shame them into behaving properly rather than modeling the kind of grace that will change them radically and permanently. Grace allows people to make choices and assumes they'll make the best choice. Grace is free and flowing and unencumbered by guilt or shame or fear, for true grace says, "I know all about you, and I still love you with a godly acceptance."

We see this in John 4, when Jesus meets the woman at the well. When she offers to give him a drink, he says, "If you knew the generosity of God and who I am, you would be asking me for a drink, and I would give you fresh living water" (John 4:10 MSG).

Note that he talks about how gracious God can be. Yet most of us, if we were gut honest, function as if God were stingy with his grace. We fear his punishment, in the sense that we think he's the high school principal walking the halls, taking down names. Who did what and who's to blame?

But God already knows who did what and who's to blame, and he still loves us anyway. His interest is in redeeming us, not in keeping us on the hook for our sins.

Unfortunately, many of us—Christians—live our lives as if we're still on the hook, and as if we have to keep everyone else on the hook. We use weapons of the flesh—the sarcastic comment, the angry stare—all designed to get people to straighten up and live right.

In contrast, when the woman at the well goes back to her village, she says, "Come see a man . . . who knows me inside and out" (John 4:29 MSG). Nothing is hidden from him, and yet he communicates with her in such a fashion that she leaves feeling loved and accepted. That's the aroma of grace.

Did she get away with her sins? No. They cost Jesus plenty, yet you don't see him lording it over her, or putting a guilt trip on her, or even using the time for a lecture on sexual ethics. Jesus trusts that once she is confronted with God's generosity—his grace—that she will be eager to change and conform to God's commands.

It's a classic Christian paradox, isn't it? Just when you think it's time to pull out the Law and read someone the riot act, Jesus shows by his behavior that it's better to embrace that person with a costly love.

And grace does cost. It obviously cost the Son of God everything, and for you to extend grace will cost you, just as it cost the priest his silver. In fact, one way to distinguish the difference between grace and mercy is that grace costs while mercy does not.

Mercy says, "I won't press charges." Grace says, "I not only won't press charges, I'll pay for your rehab program."

## GRACE HELPS US BECOME OTHER-CENTERED

Grace is powerfully other-focused. It gives without fear of depletion. Love, forgiveness, and mercy are handed out with no thought of exhausting the supply. Someone enveloped by grace is rooted deeply in soil next to a river that never knows drought.

The prodigal's father offers a picture of the paradox of grace.[2] The story begins with a self-centered, younger son. He requests his inheritance and then squanders all his father's hard earned money, ending up working for a pig farmer. Every time he touched a pig, the young Hebrew boy was reminded how far he was from the will of God. In a state of horrible desperation, he remembers his father and decides to return home as a slave.

What was going through his mind as he headed home? Maybe he realized what a failure he was. Or maybe he thought about the money his father gave him that he had foolishly thrown away. Possibly he feared a harsh rejection, one he was sure he deserved.

Whatever he thought, he was not prepared for his father's response!

Imagine: He sees his father's house in the distance as he shamefully shuffles home. Then he sees an unidentifiable person running toward him. Then he recognizes his father and *he prepares himself for the worst.*

The prodigal was probably bewildered by his father's loving embrace. The father's love faces off against the son's self-degradation. After a few minutes of wrestling, the son's heart is finally overcome by the father's passionate embrace. He goes limp in his father's arms unable to hold back the tears.

The father is overjoyed at the son's return. This is too much for the son. He only hopes for a job as a slave, and yet he is treated as a son despite all his filthiness. The father's extraordinary grace continues as he places a ring on his son's hand and sandals on his feet and then wraps him in an extravagant robe. Each gift is a visible sign of full son-ship.

The father completes his bountiful behaviors of grace by inviting the community to a joyous celebration of his son's return. *Rather than being embarrassed at the wayward son, the father responds with merriment.* The father's response to a rebellious son is a beautiful picture of transforming grace.

Each of us has had our prodigal experiences. Prodigal behavior is common because our heart's default setting is *trust yourself at all cost.* Self-trust is rooted in the belief that I will be more gracious to myself than God will. *Who are we kidding anyway?*

We must go to Jesus to be personally tutored in Grace 101. As we receive his grace, we can then pass his grace to others.

# 2

## BECOMING LIKE JESUS
## THROUGH HIS CALL

*"It is Jesus who calls, and because it is Jesus, Levi follows at once."*
DIETRICH BONHOEFFER

*As he walked along, he saw a tax collector, Levi son of Alphaeus, sitting in his office. Jesus said to him, "Follow me." Levi got up and followed him.*
MARK 2:14

Jesus' Objective—*To teach us that our obedient trust of
Jesus can be measured by our need to control life.*

Jesus doesn't want you to be a good person.

When he calls you to follow him, he isn't asking you to become nice and do your best at helping others. He didn't die so you could feel good about the things you've screwed-up or so you could carry a sentimental hope of being re-united beyond the grave with the people you love but who have died.

His call is a command for you to *comprehensively* and *absolutely* walk away from the way you do life now so you can follow him down an *exclusive* path through the *narrow* gate that leads to the kingdom of heaven.

The first thing you have to let go of is the illusion that following Jesus is about becoming a good person. Otherwise, you're just going to keep trying to make yourself good by following a list of Sunday school rules that are self-righteous attempts to enter the kingdom of heaven on your own power, somewhere separate and away from the *Jesus gate*.

This simply sets you up on a cycle of failure and condemnation, where you keep thinking you have to *try harder* and *do better* to please God. By following your list, you think you're doing well, but then you stumble. So you *try harder* and you actually do *do better*, but then you fail again and feel condemned for your failure. So you try harder and do better, but then you fail again.

It is a vicious cycle that we so easily slip into when we fail to grasp the grace of God or, like the Galatians, fail to remain living in his grace. We exhaust ourselves trying to follow a list of rules related to Christian conduct—what it looks like to be good—without realizing those very rules, no matter how well intentioned, will take us further away from God rather than bringing us under the shadow of his wings (Psalms 17:8).

## LEGALISM OCCURS WHEN RULES REPLACE RELATIONSHIP
Like a frog in kettle, we do not see that when our relationship with Jesus is replaced by rules, the rules then take on an inordinate and unnatural heaviness. We end up making the rules the main thing when the main thing has always been Jesus.

But the same thing can happen when we mistake the doctrine of grace for the doctrine of being nice, where following Jesus is all about "going along to get along" and a shoulder shrug of "nobody's perfect" becomes our response to sin.

The gospel of niceness has absolutely nothing to do with actual gospel truth and when we pretend they are synonymous, we become a people of lies, who show more loyalty to a sickly, sweet image of discipleship than to the real, sweaty, messy, honest, difficult discipleship Jesus requires of us.

Jesus commands that you abandon your life so that he can fill you with his own life. In order to help you become like him, he calls you to follow him on an intimate journey down a difficult path, through a narrow gate that leads to the kingdom of heaven. Jesus isn't looking for good or nice from you because the kingdom of heaven has higher standards than that.

Jesus wants to infuse you with his standards, his righteousness, but you must follow him wholeheartedly. You must transfer the faith you have in your own understanding to faith in Jesus Christ as Lord.

The sooner you understand this and stop trying to impress Jesus, the sooner you can follow him into the realm of costly grace. Stop right here and listen: Most disciples of Jesus linger here for a lifetime and never move into spiritual maturity. They settle down somewhere outside the narrow gate and choose to live like refugees from the kingdom of heaven, unable to access the power of God, unable to shift from fallen thinking and behavior to kingdom thinking and behavior.

Worse, we declare that Jesus is inadequate to bring us into the throne room of God. Every day we reveal the reality of our faith in Jesus; we reveal whether or not we believe him and we reveal what choices we have made regarding our obedient trust in God's Word.

The truth is: You are welcome in the kingdom. The bloody work of Jesus on the cross and his blessed resurrection paid the cost of your entry. He has opened the gate for you and you may enter by his grace. His grace is free but you must leave everything behind as you enter the kingdom. Jesus knows as you follow him you will discover that you have no need for many of the things you now consider important.

You will begin to believe that soon, but first you must follow.

## WE FOLLOW JESUS WITH REAL, TANGIBLE STEPS

The call of Jesus is a real and tangible command. It's not the beginning of a philosophical discussion or the opening of a doctrinal debate. It's not an abstract idea meant to guide us through the difficult times of life as we do our best at doing the right thing.

When Jesus calls Levi to follow, wrapped up in the command is both the sense of one exclusive path and becoming now and forever connected to that path. Quite literally, it is a call to become part of the road. In his brief expression, Jesus, in a sense, says, "I am the way and I am calling you into a unique and unending union with me, the one and only way."

But it is a command and Bonhoeffer notes that this forces Levi into a choice. He can obey or disobey the command, but he can't ignore it. In our negotiations with Jesus, we fail to grasp that anything other than total obedience is disobedience. There is no middle ground and our stalling, arguing, whining, and ignoring are all forms of disobedience that leave us in a state of perpetual immaturity.

In our time, we speak of a radical obedience to Christ and we mean an extreme or *fanatical* faith where someone is committed to Jesus to the exclusion of anything or anyone else. We mean someone who sacrifices everything, who irrevocably alters his or her life in order to follow Jesus. The sacrifice is so high and so extreme there is no turning back.

We are amazed by their sacrifice and we assume they are exceptional Christians, but the truth is their exceptional faith should be the norm and what passes for normal in our congregations is little more than a general focus on Jesus that allows us to remain satisfied sitting at the threshold of Christian maturity without ever entering in to the abundant life Jesus died to provide.

Bonhoeffer says we've been lulled into believing there are two tiers to discipleship—sort of like cable plans, with basic channels and a premium package for the more pious. We delude ourselves, thinking there are but a few among us—monks, missionaries, and ministers—who are called to be more saintly while the rest of us settle comfortably into a mediocre, part-time discipleship.

Jesus, in contrast, will not tolerate lukewarm, wishy-washy disciples (Revelation 3:16). Clearly, what we call radical obedience here on earth is *the obedience expected in the kingdom of heaven*.

In other words, our lukewarm discipleship is actually radical *dis*obedience. If radical discipleship is reflected by people who intimately believe Jesus *really means what he says*, then what other choice is there? A tier of discipleship for people who *think Jesus may mean what he says* but they're not sure? A tier of discipleship for people who *sort of agree with Jesus* and sort of live according to his commands?

To become a disciple of Jesus means we move from rebellion against God to communion with God. We may not understand all that discipleship involves or all that it will cost us, but Jesus calls us to take the first step, and then we will develop the additional faith necessary to take the next step.

Bonhoeffer says the road to faith begins with this real and tangible step of obedience. In other words, being a disciple of Jesus doesn't mean simply agreeing with Jesus or even heading in the same *general* direction as Jesus. It's sort of like this: You can agree smoking is hazardous to your health, but it means nothing until you stop smoking.

We're not called to follow Jesus in principle as if we were negotiating a contract and have come to an agreement in principle. We're called to sever the ties to our current lives so we can follow after Jesus into our new lives—our real lives (Colossians 3:3).

## WE FOLLOW A PERSON, NOT A PHILOSOPHY

We're not called to a confession of faith or an intellectual agreement with biblical doctrine. Those may help us understand our commitment to Jesus, but the call of Jesus is to Christ himself. Bonhoeffer teaches that we adhere to the person, the only begotten son, the author and perfector of our faith. We are called into a relationship; we cannot be servants to an abstract doctrine.

"Men pour themselves into creeds," says Oswald Chambers. "And God has to blast them out of their prejudices before they can become devoted to Jesus Christ."[3] Discipleship without Jesus is no discipleship at all, notes Bonhoeffer. "It is nothing else than bondage to Jesus Christ alone," says Bonhoeffer. "No other significance is possible, since Jesus is the only significance. Beside Jesus nothing has any significance. He alone matters."

Because Jesus is real, our response to his call must be real. We must take a concrete step into the realm of grace. "For faith is only real when there is obedience, never without it, and faith only becomes faith in the act of obedience," says Bonhoeffer. He adds, "Only the obedient believe. And we believe only when we obey a concrete command. Without the step of obedience, faith is only pious humbug that leads us into grace that isn't costly."

But taking a step in and of itself doesn't mean we obey Jesus. He is very specific in what he tells us to do. He doesn't say, "Follow some general biblical principles" or "Submit yourself to a certain doctrine." Jesus doesn't present a plan for positive thinking or suggest seven simple steps to becoming his disciple. Jesus says, "Follow me," and we follow a person.

"Discipleship without Jesus Christ is a way of our own choosing," says Bonhoeffer. "Even if our choice leads us to martyrdom, it is devoid of promise and Jesus will certainly reject it."

Jesus calls us to a level of intimacy that can only be sustained by his constant presence in our lives. He says, "Walk with me and work with me—watch how I do it. Learn the unforced rhythms of grace. I won't lay anything heavy or ill-fitting on you. Keep company with me and you'll learn to live freely and lightly" (Matthew 11:29-30 MSG).

"There is only one way of believing on Jesus Christ, and that is by leaving all and going with the incarnate Son of God," says Bonhoeffer. "We can be enthusiastic about an abstract idea; we even can put it into practice. But we can never follow an idea in personal obedience. Christianity without the living Christ is inevitably Christianity without discipleship; Christianity without discipleship is always Christianity without Christ."

"It remains an abstract idea," says Bonhoeffer, "a myth which has a place for the Fatherhood of God, but omits Christ as the living Son. And a Christianity of that kind is nothing more or less than the end of discipleship. In such a religion there is trust in God, but no following of Christ." Jesus calls us to abandon such abstract ideas of discipleship. He won't allow us to pretend Christianity is an add-on philosophy to the life we've mapped out for ourselves. To follow Jesus means we abandon all or we abandon Jesus.

The kingdom of heaven is like the man who finds hidden treasure in a field. He resorts all of his priorities because nothing is as important as buying the field. It is like the shopkeeper who finds a rare pearl and realizes everything else he has pales in comparison and so he never looks back to the things that once were important (Matthew 13:44-50). Where we have been loyal to many things, now we must be loyal to one thing: the person, Jesus Christ.

## TRUE DISCIPLES COMMIT TO JESUS

*As they went on their way, a man said to Jesus, "I will follow you wherever you go." Jesus said to him, "Foxes have holes, and birds have nests, but the Son of Man has no place to lie down and rest."(Luke 9:57-58)*

The Son of God himself commands obedience from his disciples, but he also expects us to count the cost of our commitment (Luke 14:28-30). Bonhoeffer says disciples with a romantic view of following Christ volunteer to go anywhere at any time, but romanticism withers when the commitment becomes inconvenient—or when it collides with the full cost of discipleship.

Discipleship means we give up any thought that there will be bits and pieces of our lives that can remain unaffected by our relationship with Jesus. We no longer have the choice to serve where we want in the way we want and still be home in bed by 10:00 PM. We no longer have the luxury of deciding our future based upon a 401K and a dental plan.

Can you imagine the apostle Paul deciding where to go next based on the cost of living in a particular town? Why should we be any different? We serve the same Lord; we're infused with the same Holy Spirit? Are the standards of discipleship different now than they were in the first century A.D.? Are we called to a lesser (second-tiered) discipleship? Do we serve a lesser Lord?

When we have a romantic view of discipleship, we may imagine ourselves giving up everything for Jesus as the world admires our faith and people express their heartfelt gratitude for our sacrificial service. But the cost of discipleship will likely be the scorn of a world that sees you throwing away your future to help people who can give you nothing in return. Discipleship may mean sacrificing for others who will have no appreciation for what you have done—much like Jesus, who was ridiculed as he died on a cross.

The grace to go wherever Jesus tells us to go comes only through the call of Christ and the power of God infused into our being. Grace only comes to us as we obey Jesus, regardless of the circumstances or consequences.

How much of your service to Jesus is based upon what is convenient for you and how much of it is based upon you doing what Jesus tells you to do?

## TRUE DISCIPLES FOCUS ON JESUS

*He said to another man, "Follow me." But that man said, "Sir, first let me go back and bury my father." Jesus answered, "Let the dead bury their own dead. You go and proclaim the kingdom of God." (Luke 9:59-60)*

Bonhoeffer says, "When we are called to follow Christ, we are summoned to an exclusive attachment to his person. The grace of his call bursts all the bonds of legalism. It is a gracious call, a gracious commandment. It transcends the difference between the law and the gospel. Christ calls, the disciple follows: that is grace and commandment in one."

In other words, we're called to focus on Jesus, not the law. Yet, like this disciple, we often say to Jesus, the Law-Giver, "Let me do what I'm supposed to and then come follow you." Jesus replies, in a sense, "Don't use the law as an excuse not to follow me. Don't put the law above me." We follow the law by following Jesus (Luke 14:25-26).

## TRUE DISCIPLES ABANDON TO JESUS

*Someone else said, "I will follow you, sir; but first let me go and say good-bye to my family." Jesus said to him, "Anyone who starts to plow and then keeps looking back is of no use for the kingdom of God." (Luke 9:61-62)*

When we follow Jesus, we cannot stipulate our own terms. Discipleship is not, Bonhoeffer notes, like a career we map out for ourselves: "I'll do this for Jesus after I get the kids through school and build my retirement fund." We cannot arrange things to suit ourselves; otherwise, Bonheoffer says, we end up serving Jesus "in accordance with the standards of a rational ethic."

This still leaves us in control, deciding our service on what makes sense. We may accomplish good things but that doesn't make us disciples of Jesus. Jesus says, "Anyone who starts to plow and then keeps looking back is of no use for the Kingdom of God" (Luke 9:61-62).

Looking back is double-mindedness. It makes us unstable and uncertain and that's the exact opposite of the focused following Jesus expects of us. It means there are moments in our relationship with Jesus when we say, "I'll get back to you, Jesus, just as soon as I finish with my priorities." It is the creature putting the Creator on hold.

The call of Jesus is a real command and it requires that we take a real and tangible step in response. Bonhoeffer says this first step of obedience places us in a position where faith becomes possible. Before the call, we are able to live life without faith. It may even be a good and admirable life, but it is *a faithless life*.

To follow Jesus, we must have faith—a confident intimate trust in him. We cannot follow Jesus and try to remain in our faithless life. We cannot get to where Jesus is taking us unless we have this faith in him.

## TRUST DEVELOPS THROUGH OBEDIENCE

For example, Peter was in a storm-tossed boat when he saw Jesus walking on the water. Peter thought that if Jesus would just call him, he would be able to walk on the water too. Jesus calls, but Peter still had to decide to step out of the boat. Thinking Jesus might give him the ability to walk on water is one thing, but it was quite another matter for Peter to actually trust Jesus *would* give him the ability. But the only way Peter is able to know is to step out of the boat. If his trust is well-placed, he will know for certain Jesus can do it. If his trust is ill-placed, then he will end up floundering in the water.

Peter's step from the boat—the moment he put all his weight on the water—was a moment of no return. He would either sink or walk with Jesus. But note that Peter didn't just jump out of the boat; he waited for Jesus to call him out of the boat. And then his obedience put him in a place where his faith became real.

Jesus calls us to step into a new life—a life of faith. Bonhoeffer says, "The disciple is dragged out of his relative security into a life of absolute insecurity (that is, in truth, into the absolute security and safety of the fellowship of Jesus), from a life which is observable and calculable (it is, in fact, quite incalculable) into a life where everything is unobservable and fortuitous (that is, into one which is necessary and calculable), out of the realm of finite (which is in truth the infinite) into the realm of infinite possibilities (which is the one liberating reality)."

When Peter stepped out of the storm-tossed boat and onto the water, where was the safest place to be? In the boat or in the arms of Jesus? The answer, of course, is Jesus, and for a brief time Peter saw that. Right then he got a glimpse of what it is like to intimately trust Jesus and what it is like to operate within the realm of costly grace as a citizen of the kingdom of heaven.

And we get a glimpse of that too. We see that following Jesus requires us to step into apparent insecurity in order to find true security. In the *alleged* insecurity of discipleship, we experience the gift of Christ and are enveloped in the grace of God.

## WE MUST EXERCISE FAITH FOR IT TO GROW

It is a paradox of faith: Our first step of faith places us in a position where faith becomes possible. By our obedience, we learn to be faithful. If we refuse to follow, we never learn how to obediently believe. We stay stuck in the shallow end of faith, trusting in ourselves, living by sight and not by faith.

Bonhoeffer notes that the step we take is itself inconsequential. We are saved by faith, not any action, even our step of faith. Jesus commands; we obey. You do not become a child of God through obedience, but by faith (Romans 1:17). The essence of discipleship is Jesus constantly pushing us into new situations where it is possible for us to intimately believe on Jesus as God incarnate. "It is the impossible situation in which everything is staked solely on the word of Jesus," says Bonhoeffer. He adds, "Had Levi stayed at his post when Jesus said 'Follow me,' Jesus might have been his present help in time of trouble, but not the Lord of his whole life."

It is the fallacy of cheap grace to think we can live life without faith, a faith that is founded on the truth that Jesus is the Lord of everything, large and small in our lives. And it is the fallacy of legalism that we can reduce faith to standardized steps that allow us to follow mere rules rather than immersing ourselves in the presence of Jesus and seeking our Lord's guidance constantly throughout each day. Most of the time when we are *struggling with faith*, we are actually *struggling with obedience* to Jesus.

## THINK OF GRACE AS A SANCTUARY

Why is grace costly if it is a free gift from God? Think of it like this: Grace is a sanctuary surrounded by sin as well as God's law. Outside the sanctuary, the law must destroy sin. Outside the sanctuary, the law demands perfection. No matter how good you are, if you slip just once, you have violated the law. You have sinned. Outside the sanctuary of grace, the wages of sin is death.

When you step into the sanctuary of grace, you are no longer pursued by the law. You are safe within the righteousness of Christ. You are free to live boldly, free of the fear that you might sin.

But that doesn't mean that the law no longer functions. The law continues its work outside the sanctuary. You can enter the sanctuary of grace for free; however, you cannot bring anything into the sanctuary with you. You must leave everything behind and begin a new way of living within the sanctuary of God's grace.

Inside the sanctuary, you can continue to live as if you are on the outside under the law, but that is a denial of your current reality. And it is a misunderstanding of the gift God has given you. The Apostle Paul rebuked the Galatians for thinking they still owed allegiance to the law:

"Tell me this one thing: did you receive God's Spirit by doing what the Law requires or by hearing the gospel and believing it? How can you be so foolish! You began by God's Spirit; do you now want to finish by your own power? Did all your experience mean nothing at all? Surely it meant something! Does God give you the Spirit and work miracles among you because you do what the Law requires or because you hear the gospel and believe it?" (Galatians 3:2-5)

Cheap grace is assuming you can live under God's sanctuary away from the law while remaining independent of God's desires:

*"You used to live in sin, just like the rest of the world, obeying the devil—the commander of the powers in the unseen world. He is the spirit at work in the hearts of those who refuse to obey God. All of us used to live that way, following the passionate desires and inclinations of our sinful nature. By our very nature we were subject to God's anger, just like everyone else.*

*But God is so rich in mercy, and he loved us so much, that even though we were dead because of our sins, he gave us life when he raised Christ from the dead. (It is only by God's grace that you have been saved!)" (Ephesians 2:1-5, NLT)*

## The Cost of Discipleship—

You must stop seeing Jesus as an *add on* to your life and begin seeing Jesus as the *reason* for you life. You must give up serving Jesus on the basis of common sense and begin the hard task of listening for his specific direction. You must give up sentimental thoughts of Christian goodness and service and live from the vision Jesus provides of the Christian life.

## Fallen Thinking—

- "I decide for Christ" instead of "I submit to Christ."
- I follow the teachings of Jesus, but common sense has the final say for each step I take along the way. I won't take a step unless it makes sense.
- I have brought Jesus into my current life and am in general agreement with the direction Jesus is taking me.

## Kingdom Thinking—

- "I submit to Christ' instead of 'I agree with Christ."
- I have abandoned my current life and followed Jesus into a new way of thinking and behaving. I will no longer automatically decide things based on common sense. I will ask Jesus to give me his wisdom.
- I am taking specific steps to follow Jesus. I cannot take these steps without Jesus.

## Your Choice?

Will you follow Jesus into a new life or will you try to attach Jesus to your current life? Will you take steps that require faith or will you take steps that are *faithless*?

# 3

# Becoming Like Jesus in Obedience

*"The actual call of Jesus and the response of single-minded*
*obedience have an irrevocable significance. By means of them*
*Jesus calls people into an actual situation where faith is possible."*
Dietrich Bonhoeffer

Once a man came to Jesus. "Teacher," he asked, "what good thing must I do
to receive eternal life?"

"Why do you ask me concerning what is good?" answered Jesus. "There is
only One who is good. Keep the commandments if you want to enter life."

"What commandments?" he asked.

Jesus answered, "Do not commit murder; do not commit adultery; do not
steal; do not accuse anyone falsely; respect your father and your mother; and
love your neighbor as you love yourself."

"I have obeyed all these commandments," the young man replied. "What
else do I need to do?"

Jesus said to him, "If you want to be perfect, go and sell all you have and
give the money to the poor, and you will have riches in heaven; then come and
follow me."

Matthew 19:16-21

*Jesus' Objective—To teach us that we will only develop faith*
*when we take steps that require us to obediently trust Jesus—*
*but those steps must be the ones Jesus tells us to take.*

When Jesus calls the rich young man to single-minded obedience, he
leaves no room for compromise, no middle ground, no negotiation. His

call is a quiet but firm command that the young man decide: Are you in or are you out?

Jesus will not allow the young man to mistake a good life for the God-life. We see the Lord of Life calling the young man to new life, but it is life radically different from the one he has known. It is life as God created it to be, energized by the Spirit and in intimate communion with the only begotten Son.

The young man wants to know what else he needs to do in order to have eternal life and Jesus, the author of life, says it is a very simple thing: "Give up your good life in order to live the God-life with me. There's no herculean task required, no run through the jungle, no extraordinary efforts. Just make the choice to obey me."

The choice Jesus requires isn't about the young man's possessions; it's about the things that possess him. He is a good man, but his tight grip on *things* keeps him from becoming God's man.

Jesus will not allow the young man—any more than he will allow us—to perpetuate the myth that we can get to the God-life on our own terms. He won't allow us to be double-minded in discipleship, where we agree to follow after Jesus but then get sidetracked—chasing hypothetical moral or intellectual dilemmas down trails that get us nowhere nearer righteous living, let alone into the kingdom of heaven.

## BE OBEDIENT TO THE COMMANDS YOU KNOW

Bonhoeffer suggests that our many "what ifs" about discipleship keep us from the necessity of obedience. We get so wound up trying to understand each step along the way—or, like the rich young man, trying to figure out that *one thing we must do*—that we become enslaved by doubt. Yet, our freedom is found in simple, single-minded obedience to Jesus.

We must do what we know we're supposed to do and, as we take each step of obedience, Jesus will reveal the next step. Otherwise, we end up picking and choosing which commandments to obey, and our lingering debates lull us into thinking we are in a negotiation with Jesus when, in fact, we are simply disobeying him.

Bonhoeffer writes that the rich young man is actually attempting to "preserve his independence and decide for himself what is good and evil." And that echoes back to the Garden and the hiss of the snake: "Did God really say that?" *Surely there must be more to this than what God says?* In this way, "doubt and reflection take the place of spontaneous obedience. The grown-up man with his freedom of conscience vaunts his superiority over the child of obedience. But he has acquired the freedom to enjoy moral difficulties only at the cost of renouncing obedience. In short, it is a retreat from the reality of God to the speculations of men, from faith to doubt."

Look at it this way: When para-troopers are trained to jump from a plane, they have to reach a point where they do not hesitate at the door. Otherwise, they wash out of training. They cannot approach the threshold and then decide whether or not to jump. It's not the time to debate whether the plane is at the right altitude or going the right speed. It's not the time to question if they're over the right target or if the pilot knows where he is going. It's not the time to question if they were really ordered to jump or if they should wait to jump until they're absolutely, beyond a shadow of a doubt, certain the jump will be safe.

The real question is: did you sign up to be a paratrooper or not?

If the answer is yes, then they must learn to jump without reservation or hesitation. They must trust that the plane is at the right altitude and going the right speed, that they are over the target, that the pilot knows what he is doing.

## SINGLE-MINDED OBEDIENCE TO THE MIND OF CHRIST

The question is: Did you agree to follow Jesus or not? If we want to be his disciples, we must learn to obey immediately and without reservation. Jesus commands we drop our speculations and become single-minded in our obedience to him. What if the plane is too high or not over the right target? Part of our obedient trust in Jesus is that he will work it out, "that in all things God works for good with those who love him, those whom he has called according to his purpose" (Romans 8:28).

(It should be noted that Bonhoeffer stressed immediate obedience because he saw so many people delaying and debating their response to the commands of Jesus. However, as he watched the Nazi regime abusing authority, Bonheoffer saw the distinction between blind obedience and humble obedience. In his next book, *Life Together*, he taught that obedience is best developed within a Christian community, where we are able to balance any "impulse" with the counsel of other mature Christians. Bonhoeffer's point, though, is we must do what Jesus tells us to do and not delay for ulterior purposes.)

Jesus commands us to drop our speculations and become single-minded in our obedience to his commands. In the case of the rich young man, this pulls him away from the fantasy that Christ's commands are merely "an opportunity for moral adventure, a thrilling way of life, but one which might easily be abandoned for another if occasion arose." The young man is pulled into the reality of costly grace, where the only hope to enter the kingdom of heaven lies in Jesus Christ, our Lord. Jesus won't allow him to see eternal life as a distant dream; he insists he follow him into that life now: *The kingdom of heaven is upon you.*

Discipleship, then, says Bonhoeffer, is not the completion of an old life, doing that one final thing you have to do to enter the kingdom, like the capstone of a long and distinguished career ushers you into retirement. Discipleship is about irrevocably leaving your present life behind and entering a new life, where Jesus is the center of significance.

In truth, it is a life in which Jesus is the only significance.

Bonhoeffer says, "Here is the sum of the commandments—to live in fellowship with Christ." We allow Jesus to bring us to the place where we abandon anything that holds us to the old life, anything other than Jesus to which we are attached.

## ONLY FAITH LEADS TO SECURITY

*When the young man heard this, he went away sad, because he was very rich.* (Matthew 19:22**)**

For the rich young man, the thing that held his loyalty more than anything else was his wealth. *"He was holding on tight to a lot of things, and he couldn't bear to let go"* (Matthew 19:22 MSG).

The thing that holds our loyalty may be different. For us, it may be prestige or reputation, promotion or influence, friends or family. It may be an insistence that we must earn our way into God's good graces or it may be a deeply rooted delusion that following Jesus simply means we become nice people. It may be a loyalty to cheap grace, where we think forgiveness of our sins is *de facto* permission to keep on living the way we always have. After all, Jesus forgives us.

No matter what it is, if we give it greater loyalty than we give Jesus, it is an idol and we are engaged in idolatry.

We are reluctant to give up these things that grip our attention because we think they provide us with a degree of security. In truth, what appears to be security is, in fact, insecurity—and what appears to be insecurity is, in truth, eternal security.

## THE NEXT STEP IS REVEALED AFTER THE FIRST STEP

When Jesus called Peter to step out of the boat and walk to him across the water, it was a call to voluntarily give up the security of the boat for the insecurity of walking on rough water (Matthew 14:22-31). With single-minded obedience, Peter takes the first step and, in that moment, he believes. Obedience doesn't merely reflect belief; in truth, obedience leads to belief.

God uses our obedience to put us in a position to develop faith. Jesus calls us to take the first step and then, only after we've taken that step, he will reveal the next step. In this sense, you cannot develop faith if you are disobedient to Jesus. You may give intellectual assent to what God can do, but unless you take the first step, you do not have faith.

Yet this is where so many of us get stuck. We hesitate; we step back from obedience in order to speculate what we should do next even though Jesus has already told us what we must do. There is no other path than obedience to developing faith.

Only by leaving the "security" of the boat does Peter discover that the greater security is in Jesus. In truth, the *only* security is in Jesus. Peter learns firsthand—or perhaps firstfoot!—that Jesus is Lord over all circumstances.

Peter also learns that what we see and think, apart from Jesus, do not reflect reality. The delusion is that the greatest safety is in the boat; the reality is that the greatest safety is in focused obedience to Jesus. The delusion is that we cannot walk on water; the reality is that we can do whatever Jesus commands us to do. The delusion is that the waves will overcome us; the reality is that Jesus is greater than the waves.

## DON'T LOOK AT THE WAVES; LOOK AT ME

The call of discipleship is to follow after Jesus, even onto the water. In a sense, Jesus beckons: 'Come closer to me. Be my disciple. Learn the unforced rhythms of grace. I am the only way. So I require you to be focused exclusively on me in your obedience.'

Then, to underscore the need for single-minded obedience, the Gospel account tells us that Peter became distracted. His focus comes off Jesus as he sees the wind whipping across the waves, and he begins to sink into the water. His obedience is now double-minded—and he provides a profound object lesson in what happens when we try to serve two masters.

Here is the way of cheap grace: We want to walk on water; yet, we insist on the right to focus on whatever we want—sometimes Jesus, sometimes the wind and waves; sometimes Jesus, sometimes our careers and casual pursuits; sometimes Jesus, sometimes "the sin that so easily entangles" (Hebrews 12:1 NIV).

When we choose to focus on our cares and worries, taking our focus off Jesus, we cheapen the miracle of walking on water by elevating our anxieties to the same status as the miracle. In other words, which is more important, which should demand our greater attention—the ability of Jesus to care for us or the concerns we have about our circumstances?

And so, rather than obeying the commands of Jesus, we demand he tolerate our distractions and double-mindedness. We live within a mythology that says we can somehow follow after Jesus, yet pick and choose what commandments we will obey—and when we'll obey.

But, if we want to live within grace, we must hear the voice of Jesus directing, 'Don't look at the waves; look at me.'

Is it any wonder so many disciples of Jesus are storm tossed and unstable? Costly grace calls for a single-minded focus on Jesus and simple, immediate obedience to his commands—no matter how counter-intuitive they may seem.

## ANXIETY IS THE OPPOSITE OF TRUST

Bonhoeffer uses Christ's command that we not be anxious as an example of how easily we rationalize our way out of obedience: "If [Jesus] were to say to us: 'Be not anxious,' we should take him to mean: 'Of course it is not wrong for us to be anxious: we must work and provide for ourselves and our dependents. If we did not, we should be shirking our responsibilities.'"

Yet it is a sin to be anxious because Jesus commands us not to be anxious. Jesus wants us to understand that anxiety is not just a matter of human emotion;

it may also reveal a deep mistrust of God. Instead of obediently trusting that Jesus will do what he says, we say we know better—and in the process we make ourselves God.

When we choose our anxiety over the divine promise to meet our needs, we are like a child who is constantly afraid that something is in the closet. His father checks and assures his child nothing is there; still, the child is anxious. He trusts his feelings—his fear—more than he trusts his father. The father says, "I have looked. I have checked. There is nothing there. Believe me! Stop being anxious, because you are getting yourself worked up over something that simply shouldn't be a concern."

Bonhoeffer says we rationalize our way into disobedience in the same way. He says it is like a father who tells his son to go to bed. But the son thinks, "Daddy told me to 'go to bed' but he really means I am tired. And I am tired, but I can overcome my tiredness if I go out and play." So the boy re-arranges the command of the father in order to justify what he wants to do. While asserting his independence from the father, he holds tight to the delusion that he is obeying the father.

Our rationalizations allow us to remain double-minded as we use them to side-step the single-minded obedience that Jesus commands. But our double-mindedness doesn't mean we've avoided making a decision. A non-choice means we still haven't submitted to Jesus; that is, non-obedience is just another form of disobedience to Jesus. In this sense, we have established a category of non-compliance to the commands of Jesus and this allows widespread disobedience to become acceptable behavior within our Christian congregations. Any disobedience to the commands of Jesus is a sin.

*Jesus then said to his disciples, "I assure you: it will be very hard for rich people to enter the Kingdom of heaven. I repeat: it is much harder for a rich person to enter the Kingdom of God than for a camel to go through the eye of a needle." When the disciples heard this, they were completely amazed. "Who, then, can be saved?" they asked. Jesus looked straight at them and answered, "This is impossible for human beings, but for God everything is possible."* (Matthew 19:23-26)

Jesus is always looking at the end game. He knows that time is ticking down to the final judgment and he wants as many people as possible prepared for his return. And by commanding we give him single-minded obedience, he focuses us on the things that are essential. We live with our eyes on his imminent return and our minds on kingdom thoughts.

The problem with our religious systems, our methods and formulas, is, no matter how well intentioned, they tend to lead us away from Jesus. We begin to follow them instead of following Jesus. Rather than asking him what we should do in a given situation, we begin to assume we know what Jesus would have us do.

And this takes the immediacy out of our relationship with Jesus. Instead of going immediately to him asking, "What would you have me do now?" we make choices based on our methods, formulas, and pre-conceived notions of what a Christians should do. We decide what a Christian should be and do rather than letting *Christ decide* what a Christian should be and do.

This puts Jesus in a position of having to fight against us, dismantling our religious formulas and clearing the path into the kingdom of heaven. He knows it is impossible for us to be perfectly obedient. He knows we need his help, but he also knows we resist his help. The biggest lie we cling to and the last lie we usually give up is the delusion that we can some how bring an earned righteousness into the kingdom of heaven.

If we are not constantly walking in the humility of this truth, we will slip right back into the false belief that being good is somehow earning us points with God. Jesus shows his patience and amusement over this when the rich young ruler claims he's gotten the commandments right his whole life. *What else must he do?* "Well, that's really impressive," Jesus says in a sense. "But if you really want to be perfect, then go sell everything you have and give it away to the poor."

## NEVER ASSUME WHAT JESUS WILL SAY

Jesus goes straight for the rich young man's Achilles heel and he will not hesitate to aim straight for yours. He does not want to see you go down in flames at the final judgment, so he will press you in the same way he pressed the rich young man: "If you really want to be perfect, then get rid of the thing you are so attached to that keeps you from being wholeheartedly submitted to my commands."

His point is this: He wants us to stop trying to be perfect so we can see that we need him. He wants us to fall on his grace and stop trying to prove how righteous we think we are. The apostle Paul says we have to come to the end of our rope, realizing how wretched we are, before we can believe Jesus "acted to set things right in this life of contradictions where [we] want to serve God with all [our] heart and mind, but [are] pulled by the influence of sin to do something totally different" (Romans 7:25 MSG).

## A STEP OF FAITH REQUIRES FAITH

What Jesus is trying to do, says Bonhoeffer, is to move us into "an actual situation where faith is possible." It is a place where we take a step of faith that is irrevocable, a step that makes us totally dependent upon Jesus. Our decision to follow Jesus, then, becomes as irrevocable as the rich young man giving away all his wealth. His life will never be the same; he is totally dependent upon Jesus. He would be in a place where he would see and experience—daily, even minute-by-minute—that the promises of Jesus are true. Or he would discover that Jesus in unable to deliver.

And, whether the promises are true or not, the rich young ruler cannot go back. Neither can we if we walk by faith. "We are not people who turn back and are lost. Instead, we have faith and are saved; for our life is a matter of faith, not of sight" (Hebrews 10:39; 2 Corinthians 5:7).

When we draw back from this threshold of faith, we are assuming Jesus will not or cannot deliver. Bonhoeffer says this is where most of us stumble in our walk of faith. We agree in our head that something needs to change in our lives. In the sense of contracts, we agree, in principle, to follow Jesus. But that is not faith; in truth, it creates the kind of faithless Christianity that is prevalent in so many congregations. We end up being relatively good people trying to live good lives; but that has nothing to do with following Jesus down the hard path through the narrow gate into the kingdom of heaven.

Doing our "best" and trying hard merely to be good people doesn't require a serious accounting of our sins and it doesn't require what Oswald Chambers refers to as the *maimed life*,[4] where we truncate our own desires in an irrevocable, single-minded obedience to Jesus—whatever God wants of my life I will do no matter what it costs me. Generic goodness actually works against us because it never demands we declare, "Oh, what a wretched man or woman that I am," which the apostle Paul says is essential to our transformation from the old life into the new (Romans 7:24).

It is just another form of cheap grace that doesn't require a real, tangible, trusting step of faith so inherently significant that our lives are irrevocably changed.

This is why it is so rare to see people with radically altered lives. This is why, if the truth be told, we think of someone wasting his or her life if they chase after something less than the fantasies we create of how things ought to be. For instance, the brilliant doctor who follows the call of Jesus to an obscure life serving one tiny village, or the athlete who passes on a professional contract to live in poverty as a missionary. Responses like these to the call of Jesus should be the norm, but we have made them the exception. And that's not the way we will think in the kingdom of heaven.

"By eliminating simple obedience on principle, we drift into an unevangelical interpretation of the Bible," Bonhoeffer says. "We take it for granted that as we open the Bible, we have a key to its interpretation. We no longer depend on God for the answers and understanding, depending instead on our principles of understanding."

"We are one step removed from God by a law," says Bonhoeffer. "The principle stands between us and our Father, when the only thing that is supposed to stand between us and God is Jesus Christ." Bonhoeffer's issue is not that we cannot use biblical principles for teaching; the problem occurs when people elevate biblical principles above the Word of God, who is Jesus. Jesus commands; we obey him, not the principles.

Legalism, on the one hand, establishes biblical principles as law, eliminating the need for intimacy with Jesus. Cheap grace, on the other hand, employs biblical principles as guidelines, eliminating the responsibility to adhere to the commands of Christ in any and all situations. The point is, we should never let a list of rules or principles come between us and our intimate relationship with him.

## JESUS DETERMINES WHAT FAITH-STEP WE SHOULD TAKE

Bonhoeffer stresses that "Obedience to the call of Jesus never lies within our own power." We cannot decide what the step is that will bring us into greater faith; only Jesus can decide that. He calls; we follow, and that is why we are responsible for listening to him and doing just what he says. In addition, our faith is not developed or deepened as the result of something we do independent of Jesus' call.

"If, for instance, we give away all our possessions, that act is not in itself the obedience Jesus demands," says Bonhoeffer. "In fact such a step might be the precise opposite of obedience to Jesus, for we might then be choosing a way of life for ourselves, some Christian ideal, or some ideal of Franciscan poverty. Indeed, in the very act of giving away his goods a man can give allegiance to himself and to an ideal and not to the command of Jesus."

Jesus knows what he is asking is impossible if we try to do it on our own, *but for God everything is possible*. He calls us to follow in obedience, and in our obedience, we will believe.

## THINK OF GRACE AS AN ORCHESTRA

Grace is an orchestra you are invited to join. Your membership is free. It is a gift from the maestro who sees a talent in you no one else sees. But joining the orchestra will cost you everything because you have to leave other things behind as you focus on following the maestro and becoming the musician God made you to be.

The maestro will demand you give up anything that distracts, anything that hinders your progress, any habit or attitude that simply isn't fitting for the grand performance to come. The maestro will not compromise in his standards of excellent; yet, every day he will be by your side, encouraging you in your development as a musician.

When some join the symphony, they refuse to give up their presumptions of what it is like to play in the orchestra. Instead of following the maestro, they follow their own formulas for how the music should be played. This is legalism and it is as much disobedience to the commands of Jesus as the rebellion we so easily cite as disobedience.

Yet, others join the orchestra and assume they don't have to work hard at becoming better musicians. They remain sloppy in their technique and they bring their bad habits into the symphony. They have no regard for the gift the maestro gave them when he invited them to join the orchestra. Some of them assume they were invited to join because of their talents and abilities, not realizing they are only there by the word of the maestro. This is cheap grace and it assumes we need not put serious effort into following Jesus with an abandonment that includes throwing off "everything that gets in the way" including "the sin which holds on to us so tightly" as we "run with determination the race that lies before us" (Hebrews 12:1).

### The Cost of Discipleship—

You must give up your double mindedness and give a singular focus to following Jesus into the kingdom of heaven. You must quickly and tangibly obey the commands of Jesus and give up the distracting debates that keep you from doing what Jesus has already told you to do.

### Fallen Thinking—

- My delayed obedience is a matter of prudence; I demand that I understand everything before I am obedient.
- My "arrangement" with Christ is conditional, based on what makes sense to me.
- I will integrate Christ and his Word into my life (rather than integrating my life into Christ and his Word), but I will only do this so long as it takes me where I want to go.

### Kingdom Thinking—

- Obeying Jesus is the safest, smartest thing I can do. When I am obedient to him, I can rest in his grace and protection, knowing he goes before and behind me.
- My delayed obedience is a faith issue I need to resolve. "Through [Jesus]we received both the generous gift of his life and the urgent task of passing it on to others who receive it by entering into obedient trust in Jesus. You are who you are through this gift and call of Jesus Christ!" (Romans 1:5-6 MSG)

### Your Choice?

Will you be shaped by Jesus as you adhere, not only to his commands, but to him personally? Or will you try to shape him into you?

# 4

## BECOMING LIKE JESUS IN SUFFERING

*"Jesus says that every Christian has his own cross waiting for him, a cross destined and appointed by God. Each must endure his allotted share of suffering and rejection."*
DIETRICH BONHOEFFER

*Then Jesus began to teach his disciples: "The Son of Man must suffer much and be rejected by the elders, the chief priests, and the teachers of the Law. He will be put to death, but three days later he will rise to life." He made this very clear to them. So Peter took him aside and began to rebuke him. But Jesus turned around, looked at his disciples, and rebuked Peter. "Get away from me, Satan," he said. "Your thoughts don't come from God but from human nature!" Then Jesus called the crowd and his disciples to him. "If any of you want to come with me," he told them, "you must forget yourself, carry your cross, and follow me. For if you want to save your own life, you will lose it; but if you lose your life for me and for the gospel, you will save it. Do you gain anything if you win the whole world but lose your life? Of course not! There is nothing you can give to regain your life. If you are ashamed of me and of my teaching in this godless and wicked day, then the Son of Man will be ashamed of you when he comes in the glory of his Father with the holy angels."*

MARK 8:31-38

Jesus' Objective—*To teach us to that suffering develops in us an obedient trust in God, where we understand God always has our best in mind even when we cannot see what he is doing. Suffering forces us into the other-centered thinking of the kingdom of heaven and pushes us into the very heart of God.*

When Jesus calls you, he expects you to begin thinking like him. This isn't as impossible as it sounds because the apostle Paul says you have been given the mind of Christ: "As the scripture says, 'Who knows the mind of the Lord? Who is able to give him advice?' We, however, have the mind of Christ" (1 Corinthians 2:16).

The issue is in accessing the mind of Christ as you mediate upon God's Word and listen to the Holy Spirit, who is your guide into all truth (John 16:13). If you imagine discipleship as a physical journey, then you can easily see that the more time you spend with Jesus, the more you will begin to understand his way of thinking.

As you walk with him day in and day out, you will become intimate with his likes and dislikes; you will see what he sees and hear what he hears. You will know what he cares about and what he considers insignificant, petty, or distracting. You will witness how he responds to problems, criticism, exhaustion, expectations, disappointments, hunger, love, laughter, accusations, sorrow, sin, rejection, legalism, religion, hypocrisy, happiness, joy, and you will learn what he thinks about your future.

You will learn to think from God's perspective, to engage the mind of Christ available to you through the Holy Sprit. In *The Message*, Eugene Peterson paraphrases the yoke of Jesus like this: "Walk with me and work with me—watch how I do it. Learn the unforced rhythms of grace. I won't lay anything heavy or ill-fitting on you. Keep company with me and you'll learn to live freely and lightly" (Matthew 11:29-30 MSG).

The apostle Peter shows how this transformation takes place. As he follows Jesus, he begins to submit his mind to the Father and that changes, not only the way he thinks, but also his perspective. He begins to see things as they appear inside the kingdom of heaven. In other words, Peter begins to clearly see reality and he is able to see the truth that Jesus is the Messiah. Jesus says, "For this truth did not come to you from any human being, but it was given to you directly by my Father in heaven" (Matthew 16:17).

## JESUS MUST SUFFER AND BE REJECTED

We come to the point when we respond to the call of Jesus but then, like Peter, our discipleship breaks down when we find ourselves in disagreement with Jesus. We retreat from the reality back into the shadows of our finite thinking. In this case, Jesus explains that *he must suffer and be rejected*, but this doesn't match Peter's image of what the Messiah should be. In a sense, the apostle disengages the mind of Christ. He stops thinking like someone who lives in the kingdom of heaven and, ignoring the Father's wisdom, insists on the right to decide, not only for himself but also for Jesus.

The strong rebuke from Jesus is because Peter's insistence is nothing short of an assault on God's sovereignty. As Bonhoeffer notes, suffering and rejection are "laid upon Jesus as a divine necessity and every attempt to prevent it is the work of the devil, especially when it comes from his own disciples; for it is in fact an attempt to prevent Christ from being Christ." Bonhoeffer adds that, in suffering, Jesus bears the whole burden of humankind's separation from God. Our sin costs Jesus and, in light of his suffering, we can no longer pretend that grace is cheap. In truth, Bonhoeffer says, Jesus must not only suffer; he must also *be rejected*. Otherwise, he says, a suffering messiah may appear as something heroic and "all the sympathy and admiration of the world might have been focused on his passion." But Jesus is a *rejected* messiah and that "robs the passion of its halo of glory." He dies without honor, despised and rejected of men.

## WE BECOME LIKE JESUS THROUGH SUFFERING AND REJECTION

The cost of discipleship, then, is this: The way we become like Jesus is through suffering and rejection. Jesus became the Christ because he was rejected and suffered, and for us to become his disciples—to become like Christ—we must share in his rejection, suffering, and crucifixion.

"God is a God who bears," Bonhoeffer says. The Son of God wrapped himself in our flesh and then carried the cross even as he carried our sins straight up the hill called Golgotha. Because we are his disciples, we are called to bear for others. This is how we become like Christ. Bonhoeffer says this is "precisely what it means to be a Christian."

Jesus isn't speaking about the watered-down sort of cross-bearing we so readily accept today, where we speak of the obnoxious neighbor, the dwindling asset, or the occasional migraine as daily crosses we must bear. Bonhoeffer notes that comparing the standard "trials and tribulations" of life with the bloody death of Jesus reduces his cross to an "every day calamity" and suggests the gospel is nothing more than a means to feeling good about our circumstances.

Certainly, we're meant to bear the obnoxious shortcomings of others, the things that annoy us about them. But when Jesus says we must bear our cross daily, he means we must bear the sins of others just as he bore our sins. This is how God brings out the life of Christ planted in us by the Holy Spirit, enabling us to take the deep regrets and loss in our lives, those past and present, and view them as God's way of acquainting us with the grief, heartache, and sorrow Jesus experienced on his way to the cross. In this way, Paul says, the death of Christ is *at work in us* so that the life of Christ can be *at work in others* (2 Corinthians 4:12).

We're called to bear the sins of others—the things they do that cost us—just as Jesus bore our sins even when there was no guarantee we'd ever notice, appreciate, or even care about his sacrifice. In truth, there was no guarantee we'd even stop incurring more cost for him to bear (Romans 5:8).

## THE CROSS GIVES US THE POWER TO FORGIVE

Bonhoeffer says the only way we can "bear that sin is by forgiving it in the power of the cross of Christ in which [we] now share." He says forgiving others is the Christlike suffering we are called to bear and this requires another shift in our thinking because it destroys any fantasy that forgiveness is all about "being nice" and "can't we all just get along."

Forgiveness is a work that costs, not only the life of Jesus, but your own life as well: "For if you want to save your own life, you will lose it; but if you lose your life for me and for the gospel, you will save it." Grace is free but it bloody-well isn't cheap. If every time we sinned, we could hear the clank of hammer to nail through wrist, the devil would have a harder time selling us on his inventory of sin.

It is bearing the sins of others, even when it means suffering and rejection, that creates the distinction between "an ordinary human life and a life committed to Christ," says Bonhoeffer. To echo the apostle Paul, "We can understand someone dying for a person worth dying for, and we can understand how someone good and noble could inspire us to selfless sacrifice," but to forgive others, even when it means suffering and rejection, who could do that but someone compelled by the power of God? (quoted section from Romans 5:7 MSG)

## JESUS CALLS US TO REDEMPTIVE ENDURANCE

And how do we know what kind of cross we are meant to bear? You will find out as soon as you begun to follow Jesus and share in his life, says Bonhoeffer. It is not a cross you can pick, but it is the one God can use to prepare you for life in the kingdom of heaven.

As we learn to think like Jesus, Bonhoeffer says our perspective on suffering and rejection will change from fearful avoidance to redemptive endurance. We will come to understand that enduring the cross is not a tragedy; rather, it is the fruit of "an exclusive allegiance to Jesus Christ."

In that light, any rejection of suffering by a disciple means the rejection of Jesus. When we avoid suffering and rejection, for instance, by chasing after little gods of compromise, we are denying Christ no less clearly than when Peter, standing next to the servants of Caiaphas by the courtyard fire, insisted he was not a disciple of Jesus.

Jesus always brings us to a choice as he watches the doomsday clock count down. The road is hard and the gate is narrow into the kingdom of heaven. Are you willing to suffer? Are you prepared to be rejected? The student is not greater than the master and the master is calling you to follow him into the kingdom, regardless of the suffering and rejection this may bring.

And why should we do that? Because the suffering of Jesus is redemptive. It leads us into an intimate and eternal communion with God, where we can approach the throne of grace boldly and with confidence. When we share in that suffering, we are pulled deeper into the heart of God. "Just as Christ maintained his communion with the Father by his endurance, so his followers are to maintain their communion with Christ by their endurance," says Bonhoeffer.

If suffering and rejection lead to intimacy with the Father, could it be the inability of so many of us to go deeper with God lies in our fear of suffering and rejection? Is it possible our avoidance of these things keeps us in the shallow waters of discipleship?

*He went a little farther on, threw himself face downward on the ground, and prayed, "My Father, if it is possible, take this cup of suffering from me! Yet not what I want, but what you want." Once more Jesus went away and prayed, "My Father, if this cup of suffering cannot be taken away unless I drink it, your will be done."* (Matthew 26:39, 42)

Jesus prays for the cup of suffering to pass, and Bonhoeffer observes that it does pass, but only after Jesus has gone through the suffering. His suffering is not permanent but, for the joy set before him, Jesus "endured the cross, scorning its shame, and sat down at the right hand of the throne of God" (Hebrews 12:2 NIV).

Jesus obediently trusted God to fulfill his promises, obediently trusted his suffering would end, and obediently trusted his suffering not only served a purpose, but would also lead to the end of suffering: "He will wipe away all tears from their eyes. There will be no more death, no more grief or crying or pain. The old things have disappeared" (Revelation 21:4).

## GOD IS NOT SURPRISED WHEN WE SUFFER

When we suffer, we can cling to the truth that God is not surprised. We do not suffer outside the sovereign power of God. We can rest in his promise that he has our best interest at heart and, when suffering and rejection come, we can obediently trust that our suffering is not an accident but a necessity as God lovingly squeezes out of us the things we might otherwise ignore or excuse—the sin, disobedience, and apathy that will get us flagged by security at the gates of the kingdom of heaven.

Once again Jesus brings the disciples to a choice. He will not force them to suffer: "If any of you want to come with me . . ." (Mark 8:34). They can follow him or choose not to, and in that sense reject him.

And this is why Jesus so often addresses the weary and broken-hearted. 'Come to me if you are desperate because only desperate men and women are willing to suffer for my cause.' They alone understand God will give them "treasures of darkness and riches from secret places, so that you may know that I, the Lord, the God of Israel call you by your name" (Isaiah 45:3 HCSB).

"Thus it begins," says Bonhoeffer. "The cross is not the terrible end to an otherwise God fearing and happy life, but it meets us at the beginning of our communion with Christ. When Christ calls a man, he bids him come and die."

Bonhoeffer notes that our death—the way we join with the death of Jesus; the way we carry his death within us (2 Corinthians 4:10)—may be leaving the home we love or a job that has become comfortable, very much like the first disciples did to follow Jesus. Or it may be leaving the comfort and predictability of our religious traditions, such as when the monk Martin Luther left the monastery.

Regardless, it is the same death every time. We die to the old life in order to live in the new life of costly grace (Romans 6:1-14). We die to our own desires and demands. "Every command of Jesus is a call to die," says Bonhoeffer. Every day we are given a choice to obey or not to obey Jesus as we face off with sin and the devil.

✥

### The Cost of Discipleship—

Suffering signals that God is near. Rather than avoiding it, I will pay the cost of suffering, knowing it draws me into the heart of the Father and that he will use it for his redemptive purposes.

### Fallen Thinking—

- My suffering is arbitrary and disconnected from God.
- Suffering is a distraction from my real purpose.
- I must avoid suffering at all costs; it has nothing to do with my commitment to Christ.
- God would not want me to suffer or be unhappy.
- Since I am suffering, I must be out of God's will. I am suffering so much; God must have abandoned me.

### Kingdom Thinking—

- The cross did not just happen to Jesus; it was part of his purpose for coming to earth.
- Suffering does not happen upon me; it is part of God's purpose for my life.
- I can face suffering knowing God uses it to squeeze me into the image of Jesus.
- The cross was not a tragedy for Jesus; it is his greatest glory.
- Just as his suffering was redemptive, my suffering will also be used by God for good.

## Your Choice?

Suffering is a critical part of the intimacy of obedience. It will push you so close to Jesus you will be able to see his loving nature and know, no matter what, that you can trust him to look out for you. Will you obediently trust the Word of God when he says your suffering leads to joy or will you place more trust in your own opinions? Will you obey Jesus even if it means you will suffer and be rejected? Or will you limit your obedience only to situations that keep you comfortable? When you suffer will you see God's hand at work and trust that his nature is good?

# 5

## BECOMING LIKE JESUS IN OUR LOYALTY

*"For the Christian the only God-given realities are those he receives from Christ. What is not given us through the incarnate Son is not given us by God. What has not been given me for Christ's sake, does not come from God. When we offer thanks for the gifts of creation we must do it through Jesus Christ, and when we pray for the preservation of this life by the grace of God, we must make our prayer for Christ's sake."*

DIETRICH BONHOEFFER

*Those who come to me cannot be my disciples unless they love me more than they love father and mother, wife and children, brothers and sisters, and themselves as well.*

LUKE 14:26

Jesus' Objective—*To teach us that, because the life of Christ flows from him through us to others, in a conflict of loyalties, Jesus must always gets the higher priority*

The call of Jesus isolates us from family and friends, nationality and tradition—and that is exactly how God intends it. Jesus calls you, not a group. He requires that you stand alone before him in an intimate, face-to-face relationship.

You are responsible for your own decision to follow him or not to follow. You are responsible for your own obedience or disobedience. Absolutely no one can stand between you and Jesus and that is why he sounds so stern when he says, "You cannot be my disciple unless you love me more . . . ."

There is a totality in discipleship that demands an uncompromising loyalty. Jesus will not share your affection for him with anyone else, not even your own family. If you are faced with a choice between loyalty to him and loyalty to your father or mother, sister or brother, you must choose Jesus or you cannot claim to be his disciple. His expectation is so strict that, when faced with a choice between the interests of Jesus and your own self-interests, you must choose for Jesus or you must admit you are not his disciple.

Think about Peter warming his hands by the fire, just before the cock crows. Will he choose for Jesus or choose for himself? A disciple of Jesus is faced with the same decision every day.

Holy Jesus meek and mild is about the serious business of salvation and he has no time for split loyalties or uncertain commitments. Any relationship you have that jeopardizes your relationship with Jesus must be sacrificed. His command may seem unreasonable; yet Oswald Chambers says we should never try to interpret these words separate from the Son of God who spoke them.

For the follower of Jesus, there is no turning back. Christ stands in the way, wrapping us in his realm of grace, insisting he be the center of our new existence.

## THINK SMALL AND TRAVEL LIGHT

His command that we break—in totality—with our old existence is not arbitrary or random. You could say it is meant to make us small enough to fit through the narrow gate that leads into the kingdom of heaven. Imagine trying to go down a narrow path and then through a narrow gate wearing a backpack overstuffed with heavy regrets from the past and superficial distractions from the present. You'd end up exhausted and frustrated as your backpack and the things spilling out of it kept getting snagged on the narrow sides of the path. You'd begin to see many of the things you carried were a hindrance rather than a help and one-by-one you'd start tossing them aside.

How would you feel when you got to the end of the path and found out the only way you could fit through was to leave everything you still had with you behind, even your backpack? So you reluctantly throw it off and head through the gate only to discover that everything you'd been carrying, *everything you'd been so reluctant to leave behind*, would have been useless in your new life in the kingdom of heaven.

Once inside the kingdom of heaven, you'd realize you'd made your journey more difficult than it had to be simply because you kept trying to hold on to things that were impossible to keep. This is why Jim Elliot, who was killed while attempting to evangelize the Waodani people in Ecuador, wrote, "He is no fool who gives up what he cannot keep to gain what he cannot lose."[5]

In contrast to what we often think, Jesus is not trying to take good things away from us when he commands our allegiance; rather, he has the end in mind. He knows the world is coming to an end and nothing we insist on keeping will survive. We think of Jesus as our Savior because he died on the cross and rose to the Father's right hand, but his task as Savior includes clearing a path for us to follow into the kingdom of heaven.

We believe Jesus is the path, the way to the Father. We believe his death and resurrection created the bridge for us to cross into the kingdom of heaven. But he also clears the path by insisting that we adhere exclusively to him, that we "rid ourselves of everything that gets in the way, and of the sin which holds on to us so tightly" (Hebrews 12:1). So "Jesus demands greater allegiance than any dictator that ever lived," says Vance Havner, the late straight-talking Baptist preacher. "The difference is that Jesus has a *right* to it!"[6]

## ENDGAME: LOVE STAYS TRUE TO ITS MISSION

He appears ruthless as he commands that you give preference to him over anyone else, including the greatest love of your life, your best friend, your romantic dreams, even your own mother. But we misunderstand Jesus if we think what appears to be ruthlessness emerges from mean-spiritedness, self-interest, or even callous insensitivity. Jesus has the endgame in mind and he wants us with him in heaven, so he insists we re-center into his image—because that is the shape of the narrow gate—the tight fit we must go through into the kingdom of heaven.

But God wants us to learn that truth is never defined by appearances. God tells us that he knows what he is doing; his plans will "bring [us] prosperity and not disaster, [they are] plans to bring about the future [we] hope for" (Jeremiah 29:11). But notice God already knows we may view his plans as a disaster, as something evil. If God didn't know we would misunderstand parts of his plan, then there'd be no need to tell us he was planning the future we hope for in the kingdom of heaven. We must obediently trust God's character and look beyond our circumstances to him.

We will change as we obediently trust in Jesus to look out for us and, as we walk in this trust, we will see Jesus consistently come through for us one time after another. Through this we see he not only keeps his promises, but he is powerful enough to keep his promises, and that helps us obediently trust him more as the risks we must take in faith increase. We come to the point where we know with confident certainty that he will be there on the other side of our step of faith.

The key to change is not working through a list of behaviors, although that certainly can help. We are changed by getting to know Jesus. He is the power to change us (Romans 4:21; Romans 1:16-17; 1 Corinthians 1:17-19). Our job is to rest in his costly grace (Hebrews 4:8-11).

Just as a man leaves his mother and father in order to be united with his wife, you are leaving all your other relationships in order to be united with Christ (Ephesians 5:31-32). It is understood that the man will never relate with others in the same way. He must abandon his former lovers. He must stop running off any time his single friends call. He must become a mature adult and stop letting his parents run his life. He must see himself as a unit, one with his wife.

## WE ARE "ONE WITH CHRIST"

Jesus is the mediator between you and God. Your intimacy with him allows you to be intimate with God, but you cannot disconnect that intimacy when you interact with others. You are a unit of "one with Christ" and so, as Bonhoeffer explains, Jesus is not only the mediator between you and God, he also becomes the mediator between you and other people—and between you and reality.

The cost of discipleship is that from now on the only way you can relate to anyone is as "one with Christ." This doesn't mean merely making others aware you are connected to Christ; it means, to echo C. S. Lewis, from *Mere Christianity*, recognizing the reality that each person you relate to is an eternal being who will spend eternity in one of two places: the kingdom of heaven or the dungeons of hell.

Your ability to love others, to respond to them as eternal beings, comes from your connection with Jesus (1 John 4:11–12). When you try to relate with them in any other way, you are trying to relate as if you are no longer connected to

Jesus. And when you do that, you're no longer leaning on Jesus as mediator and following him as a disciple.

When we buy into cheap grace, we assume, since we are forgiven, that we can now go back and relate to others as if we are not connected to Jesus. But we can't do that anymore than someone who's just gotten married can go back to former lovers and try to maintain a relationship with them that does not recognize the marriage. We are in union with Jesus just as a married man and woman are in union with each other.

When we try to separate Jesus from our relationships, we deny the reality that the life of Christ is active within us. Since that life flows from Jesus through us to others, we actually have to block the flow in order to hide Jesus from our friends, family, or business associates. And this undermines the authenticity of those relationships.

Bonhoeffer adds that the world is full of little gods who want to retain their hold over us and that is why the world is so bitterly opposed to Christ. Some of those little gods are us—we refuse to relinquish our independence from Jesus, insisting we can receive forgiveness but then return to a life of independent living.

## SEE WHAT JESUS SEES

To understand Jesus, particularly when his commands seem almost counter-intuitive—such as requiring you to love him more than your mother or brother or spouse—you have to see what Jesus sees. "Since the whole world was created through him and unto him (John 1:3; 1 Corinthians 8:6; Hebrews 1:2), he is the sole Mediator in the world," Bonhoeffer says. The world is winding down and he wants you and everyone connected to you to join him in the kingdom of heaven. There is no time for reindeer games or dangerous delusions. It is time to face the truth and live according to truth.

Yet we're not to do this in a legalistic manner—far from it actually. It's the Holy Spirit who does all the work. He is the one who leads us in truth. He is the one who helps us accomplish his work, in his truth. Jesus says, "When he, the Spirit of truth, comes, he will guide you into all truth" (John 16:13a NIV).

This makes Jesus the mediator between us and reality. We think of reality as all we see or can measure, but that simply isn't true: "To have faith is to be certain of the things we cannot see" (Hebrews 11:1). In fact, Bonhoeffer argues, the very thing we call reality is the illusion and, as long as we claim it as reality, we will find it difficult to move into the kingdom of heaven.

We struggle to see the Bible as practical or relevant when the truth is, it is infinitely practical and relevant. We are the ones who make it impractical and irrelevant by making the gospel more complicated than it is.

Bonhoeffer notes, "The call of Jesus teaches us that our relation to the world has been built on an illusion. All the time we thought we had enjoyed a direct relation with men and things. This is what had hindered us from faith and obedience. Now we learn that in the most intimate relationships of life, in our kinship with father and mother, brothers and sisters, in married love, and in our duty to the community, direct relationships are impossible."

## HEAR THE VOICE OF JESUS IN YOUR CIRCUMSTANCES

He is the reality, the practical, the relevant and we begin to see all other things through him. If we see Christianity as an ideal, then, of course, it is foolish to make kingdom living a priority. Why waste our lives on a dream, on the "impractical" and the "irrelevant."? But when you see things as they are, then you see that nothing apart from Jesus is relevant and practical. And that changes everything about the way you live.

Even the way we relate to our families—apart from Jesus—is impractical and impossible. This is why we have so much dysfunction. This doesn't mean people can't have loving, supportive families apart from Jesus. As bad as we are, we know how to give good things to our children, but how much more, then, will our Father in heaven give good things to those who ask him! (Matthew 7:11) The point is, God's design is for Christ to be at the center of all our relationships and that is the Creator's design for how we should live together.

And with kingdom eyes, suddenly that cranky spouse becomes an eternal being you must love and respect. In a sense, your spouse, your children, become the voice of Jesus calling you to be more Christlike in your relationship with them. Will you put up with the situation or compromise within the situation? Or will you learn to love your spouse into the kingdom of God; will you see the long-term consequences of your relationship?

Our break with the world may be either open or hidden. Abraham, the great patriarch of the Old Testament, left his family, friends, and country to become a

stranger in a strange land. It's easy to see his break with the world as he followed
God's promise into a new country and a new life. At times, our breaks are that
distinct, that easy to see—like the drug dealer who meets Christ and turns away
from his life of crime or the woman who breaks it off with her live-in boyfriend
because she now belongs to Jesus. Those breaks are clean and seen clearly by all
who know us.

But other times our break with the world is less obvious to others—as
when we finally *know that we know that we know* Jesus is true to his testimony.
When we make this inward break, we're no longer vulnerable to peer pressure
because we are now "certain in our uncertainty," a phrase Oswald Chambers
uses in *My Utmost for His Highest*: "We are uncertain of the next step, but we
are certain of God."[7]

Bonhoeffer says, "Outwardly, the picture is unchanged, but the old is passed
away, and behold all things are new. Everything has had to pass through
Christ." And eventually the internal becomes the external. Abraham believed
God, but, as Bonhoeffer notes, "Abraham must learn that the promise does
not depend on Isaac, but on God alone." To teach this to Abraham, God asked
him for the very relationship he treasured most. All his hopes and dreams
were wrapped up in Isaac, but what probably made the command even more
confusing was that Abraham was already committed to God's plan and trusted
in his promises.

To return to the backpack illustration, Jesus calls us to toss aside everything we
carry in the backpack, and then to toss aside the backpack as well. The backpack
is a symbol that we are carrying something to God, some good thing that will
count as righteousness for us. Jesus says the only righteousness you bring into
the kingdom of heaven is his—the righteousness he gives you.

When Abraham lifted the knife to sacrifice Isaac, he was uncertain of what
God was doing, but he was certain that God knew what he was doing. And when
God revealed the ram for sacrifice, Isaac came off the altar, no longer the pride
of Abraham's seed, but the promise of a future nation based singularly on God's
provision. And that changes everything. Abraham had no claim on how God
fulfilled his promise and we must enter the kingdom of heaven just as destitute
in our self-sufficiency.

## JESUS CALLS US TO COMMUNITY CENTERED IN HIM

While Jesus calls each of us as individuals, he draws us into a fellowship that has an eternal perspective, into a love that's real. Self-interest, manipulation, and fear no longer dominate us. We can now be who we are and our brothers and sisters can be who they are.

The One who makes us real and whole as individuals is also the founder of a new fellowship, a new community. He stands in the center between my neighbor and me—either uniting or dividing.

Though we all begin to walk the disciple's path alone, we don't remain alone. Once we take Jesus at his word and dare to be who he made us to be, our reward is the fellowship of the church—the true community where we finally become who we were made to be.

Paul says grace is a mystery, hard to explain, but perhaps we catch a glimpse of it in marriage (Ephesians 5:31-32). When you marry, you leave your old life behind and begin a new life that is other-centered. You become one with another and all of your relationships are changed because you now live within this marriage (live within grace).

It is expected that you will throw away the proverbial little black book that lists the people you have been dating or wanted to date. It is expected that you will relate to the opposite sex in a different way. You are no longer single; you are married. You belong to another; in truth, you are joined to the other. You are one with the other.

You will also relate differently to your same gender friends. It is expected that you won't just take off and do what you want. You are one with another. You communicate and coordinate together.

This is what our relationship with Jesus is meant to be like. We are in union with him. We are one with him in a similar way that a husband and wife are one. We cannot relate to other people in the same way we did before we became joined with Jesus. Even the way you relate to your mother, or father, or sister, or brother, must change, which is why Jesus says, "Those who come to me cannot be my disciples unless they love me more than they love father and mother, wife and children, brothers and sisters, and themselves as well" (Luke 14:26).

We may think we have the option, but the reality is we cannot relate to anyone as if we are separated from Jesus. We may think we can by compartmentalizing our relationships. You can't say, "Jesus is part of my life." Or, "Jesus is important to my life." You now say, "Jesus defines my life."

⁂

### The Cost of Discipleship—

We can measure our obedient trust in Jesus by looking at who gets our highest loyalty. If there is anyone other than Jesus at the top of the list, the cost of discipleship is subjugating that relationship to Jesus. Jesus must be at the top of our loyalty list.

### Fallen Thinking—

- There are Jesus things and secular things. I can keep them separate.
- I might miss out on something if I'm committed exclusively to Jesus.

### Kingdom Thinking—

- In a conflict of loyalties, Jesus always gets the higher priority.

### Your Choice?

Will I chose Jesus or will I chose the other person? Will I give Christ pre-eminence in everything: "He is the first-born Son, who was raised from death, in order that he alone might have the first place in all things. For it was by God's own decision that the Son has in himself the full nature of God. Through the Son, then, God decided to bring the whole universe back to himself. God made peace through his Son's blood on the cross and so brought back to himself all things, both on earth and in heaven" (Colossians 1:18b-20).

# 6

## Becoming like Jesus by Developing His Character

*"They have only him, and with him they have nothing, literally nothing in the world, but everything with and through God."*

DIETRICH BONHOEFFER

*Jesus saw the crowds and went up a hill, where he sat down. His disciples gathered around him, and he began to teach them:*

*Happy are those who know they are spiritually poor; the kingdom of heaven belongs to them! Happy are those who mourn; God will comfort them! Happy are those who are humble; they will receive what God has promised! Happy are those whose greatest desire is to do what God requires; God will satisfy them fully!*

*Happy are those who are merciful to others; God will be merciful to them! Happy are the pure in heart; they will see God! Happy are those who work for peace; God will call them his children!*

*Happy are those who are persecuted because they do what God requires; the Kingdom of heaven belongs to them! Happy are you when people insult you and persecute you and tell all kinds of evil lies against you because you are my followers. Be happy and glad, for a great reward is kept for you in heaven. This is how the prophets who lived before you were persecuted.*

MATTHEW 5:1-12

Jesus' Objective—*To teach us that the characteristics of Jesus develop in us because we obediently trust God to fulfill his promises, not because we try hard to be like Jesus.*

Whern Jesus sits down to give the Sermon on the Mount, the apostle Matthew implies he took a moment to gather his thoughts. The phrase he
uses signaled to an ancient audience that the message to come would be both
powerful and personal.

It is the powerful message of a king announcing the arrival of his kingdom
and inviting all who hear his call to follow him into the kingdom. It is the personal message of a God who comes to live among us—an intimate and involved
God—leaving heaven to declare that religion can no longer be used as an excuse
for keeping distant from him.

Jesus says God is for us, not against us; he wants to bless us, not curse us, but
we must come to God on his terms, not our own.

It is a life we will live in intimate connection with the God of the universe.
*Father! May they be in us, just as you are in me and I am in you," Jesus later says.
"May they be one, so that the world will believe that you sent me. I gave them the same
glory you gave me, so that they may be one, just as you and I are one: I in them and you
in me, so that they may be completely one, in order that the world may know that you
sent me and that you love them as you love me"* (John 17:21-23).

Jesus wipes away any thoughts that we can live this life independent of God.
We are called to do things that are impossible for mere humans and so we
should expect that we will be constantly pushed into positions that require
faith. If we are living a life that does not require faith, then we are not living the
life of a disciple. If we are living a life that does not require faith, then we are
living *faithlessly*.

He calls us to a life of total dependency on him, but it is not a dependency of
weakness. If we say a man is dependent upon air, we don't consider his dependency a weakness. We understand the air sustains his life.

And this isn't just an everyman sitting on the mountain. Jesus isn't just a
teacher. Here is the God of the universe, incarnated as the Son of God, looking
across the crowd with the eyes of compassionate. The Creator looking upon his
creations, whom he loves.

He doesn't see their dependence as weakness. He sees it as strength; he sees it
as intimacy; he sees it as natural, exactly how he created them to be. And if we
had his eyes, we would see it that way too, and so he sets to work to gives us the
ability to see through his eyes.

Jesus says his kingdom comes to dethrone conventional wisdom. The entire Sermon on the Mount is a series of contrasts between institutional religion and an intimate relationship with the Father through Jesus Christ. In each segment, the perfect righteousness of Jesus exposes the self-righteousness of the Pharisees, the arrogance of all our attempts to pull heaven down to us even as we stand before the one who came to bring us up to heaven.

Jesus says the very things the religious leaders value—such as power, position, prestige, and patronage—are of no value to him but these people before him, who appear to be of no consequence, who are poor and desperate are of the highest value to him.

In a sense he says you must move from fallen thinking to kingdom thinking and this means those who appear to be losers will win in the end; those who appear to be poor are of immense wealth to me; those who are weak will become strong through me.

You cannot live in the mythology of self-righteousness any longer. You cannot cling to your delusions of being good and nice and better than most. I am here to expose the lies you believe but I am benevolent in victory. I desire mercy over sacrifice. I don't need you to jump through hoops; I need you to trust in me, and to follow.

And if you choose to follow me, this is what it will be like—

## DEPENDENT

*God blesses those who are poor and realize their need for him, for the Kingdom of Heaven is theirs* (Matthew 5:3 NLT). Jesus says we must come to the end of ourselves. We must leave behind any self-sufficiency or self-righteousness, coming to the place where we realize our only hope is in Jesus Christ, our Lord. We must be desperate for God: "You're blessed when you're at the end of your rope. With less of you there is more of God and his rule" (Matthew 5:3 MSG).

Bonhoeffer notes the original disciples did not have religious wealth, in the sense that they did not have Pharisaical prestige or position. And, as they followed Jesus, they were inexperienced in this new way. All they could do was look to Jesus every step along the way; they couldn't rely on worn-in traditions that are so easily leaned upon instead of a relationship with Jesus. They had nowhere to turn but to Jesus—and that's where Jesus wants us to be—so totally dependent on him that we have no where else to go.

And it is the disciples who are blessed, not the national leaders, Bonhoeffer notes. By removing the security and prestige of religion, they are now blessed heirs of the kingdom.

## MOURNING

*God blesses those who mourn, for they will be comforted* (Matthew 5:4 NLT). Jesus says his disciples will see the world as it is. "They see that for all the jollity on board, the ship is beginning to sink," says Bonhoeffer. "The world dreams of progress, of power and of the future" but the disciples see we are headed to judgment and Kingdom Come. The world remains clueless about what's really going on, like the man who tore down his barns and built bigger ones, but "God said to him, 'You fool! This very night you will have to give up your life; then who will get all these things you have kept for yourself?'" (Luke 12:20)

Jesus knows when our eyes are on eternity, it changes the way we live. It will help us as we mourn the darkness and decay of the world, to bear a sorrow for those who are dancing toward death instead of redemption and to "bear the suffering which comes [our] way as [we] try to follow Jesus Christ," says Bonhoeffer.

"Sorrow cannot tire them or wear them down," he says, "It cannot embitter them or cause them to break down under the strain; far from it, for they bear their sorrow in the strength of him who bears them up, who bore the whole suffering of the world upon the cross."

We will begin to see what Jesus sees and care about the things Jesus cares about. We'll see a world in need of a savior; people in desperate need of a loving Shepherd—and that should encourage us as we make our break with the world in order to join Jesus on his mission to save this world.

Jesus says, "You're blessed when you feel you've lost what is most dear to you. Only then can you be embraced by the One most dear to you" (Matthew 5:4 MSG).

## MEEK

*God blesses those who are humble, for they will inherit the whole earth* (Matthew 5:5 NLT). Jesus says his disciples will be blessed if they are humble. We are humble when we come to understand who we are and who we belong to—and who is protecting us.

Bonhoeffer notes we are a community with no inherent rights, not even the right to protect our own members in the world. We live for Jesus and we obediently trust him to protect us and our own.

This is not a position of weakness. Meekness is nothing like weakness. Meekness means we are humbly patient even when provoked. Meekness is Jesus hanging on the cross after giving up his rights to God, patiently trusting that the Father is a work,

The truth is, it takes a greater strength, one re-enforced with obedient trust, to believe God will protect our rights than it does for us to make demands about our rights. But this is the shift to kingdom thinking Jesus requires: it takes more strength to conquer in love than it does to use force or violence.

We've deliberately given our rights to God alone and so, in faith, we patiently endure, knowing for certain our Father will provide for our *inheritance*. And Bonhoeffer notes our inheritance is right before us because we have the church, brothers and sisters in Christ, who provide for us in ways money never could.

It is Jesus who provides you with food in a foreign land, based on nothing more than your the testimony that Jesus Christ lives in your heart.

## JUST

*God blesses those who hunger and thirst for justice, for they will be satisfied* (Matthew 5:6 NLT). Jesus is always aware of the endgame and he calls us to be aware of the end too. As disciples of Jesus, we are helping him bring as many people as possible into the kingdom and that means we don't have time to stop and argue about our rights and possessions.

We don't allow our rights to distract us from following Jesus. We keep doing what Jesus has told us to do and trust he will take care of the rest. We know nothing will be fully sorted out and made right until the end, so why waste our time protecting temporary positions and possessions that will keep changing until we see the return of Jesus.

"Not only do the followers of Jesus renounce their rights, they renounce their own righteousness too," says Bonhoeffer. "They get no praise for their achievements or sacrifices. They cannot have righteousness except by hungering and

thirsting for it . . . They are longing for the forgiveness of all sin, for complete renewal, for the renewal too of the earth and the full establishment of God's law."

Instead our greatest desire becomes to do what God requires, to "hunger and
thirst for righteousness (Matthew 5:6 NIV). We develop a longing for the time
when all sins will cease and all sins will be forgiven, a time when our transformation is complete and God's law is established fully in our hearts.

To follow Jesus means we grow hungry and thirsty because we are no longer
nourished on our own righteousness or the righteousness of others. Happy are
those whose greatest desire is to do what God requires; God will satisfy them
fully!" (Matthew 5:6)

## MERCIFUL

*God blesses those who are merciful, for they will be shown mercy* (Matthew 5:7 NLT).
Jesus says that what we give to others, we will also be given. Bonhoeffer notes
mercy means we risk our own reputations as we take on "the distress and humili-
ation and sin of others." Jesus fills us with "an irresistible love for the down-trod-
den, the sick, the wretched, the wronged, the outcast and all who are tortured
with anxiety."

This is the kind of love that takes on the shame of others in order to bring
them into the kingdom of heaven. We may damage our own dignity and honor
as we show mercy to publicans and sinners, but that is because we are following
Jesus, a man of no reputation.

And Jesus calls us be like him, to reflect the kingdom of heaven, where none of
us will be outcasts and where we will be covered and protected for all time by the
eternal presence of God.

## PURE

*God blesses those whose hearts are pure, for they will see God* (Matthew 5:8 NLT).
Jesus says that when our hearts are pure, God will become real to us. Bonhoeffer says this means those "whose hearts are undefiled by their own evil—and by
their own virtues too."

This is a critical concept to grasp as we journey into the kingdom of heaven:
our own virtue can keep us from fully surrendering to Jesus. We have to abandon

the image of the *nice guy* or the *supportive girl* that we hold in our heads as the image of good Christians.

These images are fantasies that keep us from becoming the image of Christ. Instead of submitting to Jesus, allowing his character to emerge from within us, we'll keep trying to impress or please others with our *niceness*. We keep submitting to a false image of who we are.

Bonhoeffer says, "The pure in heart have a child-like simplicity like Adam before the fall, innocent alike of good and evil: their hearts are not ruled by their conscience, but by the will of Jesus." With a pure heart, we become absorbed in God, not our own intentions, "even the purity of high intentions."

God becomes real to us as we remember we are created in his image and as we follow after Jesus, allowing God's Only Begotten Son to transform us into his image. We abandon the business of Martha that leaves us no time to be with Jesus and adopt the focused heart of Mary, who sits at the feet of her Lord.

## PEACEFUL

*God blesses those who work for peace, for they will be called the children of God"* (Matthew 5:9 NLT). "The followers of Jesus have been called to peace," says Bonhoeffer. "When he called them they found their peace, for he is their peace."

The peace of Jesus transcends all human understanding. It is a peace based on our confidence in God's Word; forged in his forgiveness and strengthened by the heart of a Father. Jesus goes before us, guiding us down the path of peace through the narrow gate into the kingdom of heaven (Philippians 4:7; Luke 1:79; Proverbs 3:5–6).

But Bonhoeffer notes the disciples are also called to work for peace, enduring suffering rather than inflicting it and maintaining fellowship when others might break it off. We're called to help others make peace with God, and then help them make peace with each other.

We do this by entering their lives, bringing with us the same divine love that Jesus brought into our conflict with God. It is an aggressive love that simply will not stop. As Francis of Assisi prayed, "Where there is hatred, let me sow love; where there is injury, pardon; where there is doubt, faith; where there is despair, hope; where there is darkness, light; where there is sadness, joy."

"You're blessed when you can show people how to cooperate instead of compete or fight. That's when you discover who you really are, and your place in God's family" (Matthew 5:9 MSG).

## RIGHTEOUS

*"God blesses those who are persecuted for doing right, for the Kingdom of Heaven is theirs"* (Matthew 5:10 NLT). Jesus says we will be required to do what is right and this means we will face persecution. The truth is "everyone who wants to live a godly life in Christ Jesus will suffer persecution" (2 Timothy 3:12 NLT).

Bonhoeffer notes the blessing for suffering persecution is the same as for those who are humble, perhaps a reminder that we must wait upon God's justice even if the persecution we endure is for doing the very things God requires of us.

We are blessed, not because we suffer for our own righteousness, but because we carry the righteousness of Jesus within us. "The curse, the deadly persecution and evil slander confirm the blessed state of the disciples in their fellowship with Jesus," says Bonhoeffer.

*"You're blessed when your commitment to God provokes persecution. The persecution drives you even deeper into God's kingdom. Not only that—count yourselves blessed every time people put you down or throw you out or speak lies about you to discredit me. What it means is that the truth is too close for comfort and they are uncomfortable. You can be glad when that happens—give a cheer, even!—for though they don't like it, I do! And all heaven applauds. And know that you are in good company. My prophets and witnesses have always gotten into this kind of trouble"* Matthew 5:10-12 (MSG).

Jesus calls us into a community of believers, where Bonhoeffer says, "the poorest, meekest, and most sorely tried of all men is to be found—on the cross at Golgotha." With Jesus we lose it all, but with Jesus we find it all.

Grace is a caravan traveling thorough the desert. The leader says, "Join us and I will lead you through the badlands into the land of milk and honey. You will be under my protection as we travel; you will be welcomed as one of my clan, but you will also be required to live as one of my clan. If you join the caravan, if you want my protection, I will expect you to live as we do."

### The Cost of Discipleship—

The new life within us requires a new way of thinking. The life of Christ flowing from him through us requires that we live differently with " Our lives gradually becoming brighter and more beautiful as God enters our lives and we become like him" (2 Corinthians 3:18 MSG).

### Fallen Thinking—

- I become like Jesus by trying harder to act like Jesus.
- My faith (trust) in Jesus is an intellectual concept separate from my behavior.
- My obedience to Jesus is not connected to my trust in Jesus.

### Kingdom Thinking—

- I become like Jesus by obediently trusting him.
- My faith (trust) in Jesus develops as I am obedient to him.
- "What seems to be God's foolishness is wiser than human wisdom, and what seems to be God's weakness is stronger than human strength" (1 Corinthians 1:25).
- Since I have accepted Christ Jesus as Lord, I now live in union with him. I will keep my roots deep in him, build my life on him, and become stronger in my faith, as I was taught. And this fills me with thanksgiving (based on Colossians 2:6-7).

### Your Choice?

"Since, then, you have been raised with Christ, set your hearts on things above, where Christ is seated at the right hand of God. Set your minds on things above, not on earthly things. For you died, and your life is now hidden with Christ in God. When Christ, who is your life, appears, then you also will appear with him in glory." (Colossians 3:1-4 NIV)

Will you try harder to be a Christian or will you trust Jesus to develop his characteristics in you? Will you set your heart and mind on the 'things above' (your new life in the kingdom of heaven) or you keep focused on the things below (your old life)?

# 7

# BECOMING LIKE JESUS IN INFLUENCE

*"Either we follow the call [of Jesus] or we are crushed*
*beneath it. There is no question of a second chance."*
DIETRICH BONHOEFFER

*You are like salt for the whole human race. But if salt loses its saltiness, there*
*is no way to make it salty again. It has become worthless, so it is thrown out*
*and people trample on it.*

MATTHEW 5:13

Jesus' Objective—*To teach us that our influence flows from God*
*through Jesus to us, not from power, prestige, or even personal piety.*

Because you follow Jesus, you will have influence on the whole human race. Jesus says you are salt, serving as a preservative in a world being spoiled by sin. You are salt because you are connected to Jesus and his presence in you slows down the death and decay that contaminates our planet.

Bonhoeffer notes Jesus doesn't say you have the potential to become a salty influence. If you are his disciple, then you are influential. He doesn't say you will eventually become influential. When you follow Jesus in the kingdom of heaven, his life immediately begins to flow out of you, creating a contrast with anyone still living in this kingdom of death. You are influential now.

We hear about horrible things happening every day: senseless shootings, suicide bombings, hostages held, warlords of famine, ethnic cleansing, racists and rapists, the mass murderer who seemed like such a quiet guy to his neighbors. The wonder is not that it happens; the wonder is that it isn't happening more. Only the hand of God holds back the total collapse of the world. The

supernatural saltiness flowing through you as a divine preservative keeps the
world from collapse (2 Thessalonians 2:7 NIV).

## WITHOUT YOU, THE WORLD WOULD COLLAPSE

The Beatitudes explain that the poor, ignoble and weak—the disciples of Jesus—
now sustain the earth. Without you, the world would collapse. If you are a
disciple of Jesus, you carry this responsibility. Your connection to Jesus gives you
influence, but that also makes you responsible for how you use your influence.
You cannot be a disciple of Jesus and fail to carry his influence.

This is the cost of grace. This is the cost of your connection with Jesus. This is
why Jesus tells you to count the cost before you follow him into the kingdom of
heaven. His grace is free, but he requires your whole life so he can fill you fully
with his life. You no longer "live as your human nature tells you to; instead, you
live as the Spirit tells you to" because God's Spirit lives in you (Romans 8:9-10).

And this connection transforms you into a necessary influence in your corner of
the world. Because you carry this influence, you are responsible for doing exactly
what the Spirit tells you to do. Your saltiness will combat moral decay, but it will
also awaken others to the death and decay that envelops and inhabits our world.
Your seasoning will help them to see the truth, that the whole world is groaning
under it slavery to decay, but we have a confident hope that God will set us free.

To some, your saltiness will be the sweet aroma of seasoning, but to others you
will simply magnify the stench of spoiled meat, reminding them that their own
sin produces the death and decay that they smell (Romans 8:19-25).

And your saltiness will spill into the open sores of their sin, causing them to
reject and persecute you. This shouldn't be a surprise; it is to be expected. You
carry divine life into a world overrun by death (1 John 3:13-14 NIV).

It is not a question of *if* we will suffer rejection and persecution, only a
question of *when*. As Bonhoeffer notes, "In casting out the disciples the earth
is destroying its very life. And yet, wonder of wonders, it is for the sake of the
outcasts that the earth is allowed to continue."

God keeps us salty to sustain the earth while we continue the mission of Jesus
to rescue the lost from this present evil age. Jesus called us and commissioned
us to complete this mission—his mission. God's Spirit sustains the world order,
preventing its utter collapse, to buy us time to complete the mission. The Loving

Father wants no one to face eternal destruction; his deepest desire is for all people to come to repentance. He waits patiently—holding off his wrath—so his people can complete his mission and bring into the kingdom every person who is willing to come. So Jesus confronts you with another choice.

His statement implies a command: You are the salt of the earth. Will you believe me and live accordingly? Do you believe I am telling the truth?

Those who are obedient receive the strength to intimately trust, and those who intimately trust become dependable in their obedience, that is, they are *abiding* in their obedience. When we deny our saltiness—refusing to be influential - we deny the power of Jesus in our lives. We undermine his ability to be influential through us and we become worthless stewards of the influential roles he's given us. Since our influence is worthless, like salt that has lost its saltiness, "it is thrown out and people trample on it" (Matthew 5:13).

When we try to be salt without the power of Jesus working through us, it diminishes our faith. It causes us to live faithlessly because the way we live no longer requires faith.

Should it any mystery why we are ineffective in bringing others into the kingdom? If we don't intimately believe what Jesus says about us, why should others believe what we say about Jesus?

## GOD INTENDS FOR YOU TO HAVE INFLUENCE

Our refusal to use our influence is nothing short of rebellion against God's plan of salvation and grace. We are refusing to participate in God's plan. We want the privilege of grace without the responsibility. We're unwilling—and that doesn't mean we're unable—to pay the cost of discipleship. And so we say things like, "My faith is very important to me, but I'm not obsessed with it." "I believe, but I'm not fanatical or anything like that."

Yet, Jesus says, "If salt loses its saltiness, there is no way to make it salty again. It has become worthless, so it is thrown out and people trample on it" (Matthew 5:13). Some think this means to try harder—or worse, to tell others to try harder: "Get with the program. Start acting like a Christian and start telling the world how it should live." They have completely missed the point!

You didn't become the salt of the earth by your good behavior. You didn't develop supernatural influence by keeping all the right rules. You are the salt of the earth because of your connection to Jesus. You remain influential by your re-lentless obedience to Jesus—an obedience wrapped in love: "If you love me, then obey me." Your obedience is to Jesus and not to a set of rules. When you cease to be obedient, you cease to be salt.

Our good behavior—and the example we set by keeping the rules—are nothing more than by-products of our intimate connection with Jesus. But, because we get this backwards—preaching and teaching people to focus on their behavior instead of their Savior—we have congregations full of people who deny the power of Jesus in their lives.

By consistently and systematically telling people the goal is to be good rather than obedient, we have created a Christianity without Christ. We teach people to keep the rules instead of keeping the faith. We preach an anemic Christianity that suggests behavior is more powerful than the blood of Jesus and that our righteous influence comes from the rules we keep, instead of the power of God Almighty flowing through us. This is a lie straight from the pit of hell and, by believing the lie, we lose some of our saltiness. By living the lie, we put ourselves in danger of becoming so useless that we might as well be thrown out and trampled underfoot.

We will never be good stewards of our influence until we understand who Jesus is and what he can do. We are called to obediently believe that the presence of Jesus in us is powerful enough to hold back the death and decay of this world. We are called to obediently believe that Jesus is working through us in order to preserve the world long enough for as many people as possible to enter into eternal life.

If your focus is on getting others to do what is right, rather than on obeying Jesus when he tells you the right thing to do, then you are creating a climate of rules instead of a climate of love.

Love drives out all fear because, under grace, there is no longer a fear of punishment. We are influential when we speak the truth in love, telling others that their sins will not be overlooked, but will be forgiven. Salt does not influence by fear. Supernatural influence does not flow out of legislative action or economic boycott. If we will simply be who Jesus says we are—salt—then the world will be far more convicted of sin than any demands by us for righteous behavior.

The temptation of legalism is that we will lose sight of forgiveness, but the temptation of cheap grace is pretending our sins can be overlooked. Our influence does not come by trying to make it easier to get into the kingdom of heaven. That not only cheapens grace, it also is an illusion, because we have neither the authority nor the power to lower the standards of grace.

So we end up living a lie—and teaching a lie—that deludes people into believing they can do almost anything they want and still find their way down the narrow path and through the small gate into the kingdom of heaven.

And, if we accept a saltless Christianity, can we blame those who refuse to believe? Perhaps they can smell the death and decay of this world as strongly on us as it is on them.

To be a Christian and not be an influence is the revolutionary thought. Jesus says you are the salt of the earth and that makes you normal in the kingdom of heaven.

------------

*"How impossible, how utterly absurd it would be for the disciples— these disciples, such men as these!—to try and become the light of the world! No, they are already the light, and the call has made them so."*
DIETRICH BONHOEFFER

*You are the light of the world. A city on a hill cannot be hidden. Neither do people light a lamp and put it under a bowl. Instead they put it on its stand, and it gives light to everyone in the house. In the same way, let your light shine before men, that they may see your good deeds and praise your Father in heaven.*

MATTHEW 5:13-16 (NIV)

You are the light of the world. *"The God who said, 'Out of darkness the light shall shine!' is the same God who made his light shine in our hearts, to bring us the knowledge of God's glory shining in the face of Christ"* (2 Corinthians 4:6).

When God formed the world, he said, "Let there be light!" and there was light. Now he speaks the light of Jesus into our hearts and his light shines so powerfully through us that we are like stars in the universe that point the whole human race toward real life (Philippians 2:15-16 NIV).

This is a portrait of discipleship. Jesus, who is the light of the world, re-creates us into the light of the world. We are light, not because of anything of ourselves, but because we are in a supernatural union with the light of the world. He calls us to follow after him and he says, "Whoever follows me will have the light of life and will never walk in darkness" (John 8:12).

Says Bonhoeffer: "The same Jesus who, speaking of himself, said, 'I am the light,' says to his followers: 'You are the light in your whole existence, provided you remain faithful to your calling. And since you are that light, you can no longer remain hidden, even if you want to.'"

Disciples of Jesus cannot be anything but the light. Being a disciple means understanding who you are and whose you are. Discipleship is humility in its purist sense because you are not light because of your spiritual maturity or intellectual enlightenment. You are light only because you are in union with the Light.

This means you are meant individually to be a visible witness to Jesus; it means the church is a visible community, a city set on a hill that can be seen for miles around. That city on the hill, Bonhoeffer notes, is the disciple community.

There is no option other than visibility. Bonhoeffer adds, "A community of Jesus which seeks to hide itself has ceased to follow him." And what is true of the community also is true of us individually: If we try to disappear or go unnoticed or "hide our light under a bushel," we deny the call of Jesus.

We may hide the light because we're afraid of what our connection with Jesus will cost us or because we want to get ahead and know this will require compromises. We may set the gospel aside to join with a secular movement for what Bonhoeffer calls "sentimental humanitarianism." Is it wrong to work with nonbelievers for a humanitarian cause? Of course not, but we must always remember that the sacrifice of Jesus, not humanitarianism, is the only way to pull sinful humans out of the mess we're in.

We may just as easily hide the light behind religion by focusing on a system or succumbing to legalism; yet, Jesus is the light—not Arminianism, not Calvinism, not Reformed Theology, not denominationalism, not church growth, not seminars and seminary, not civility, not nobility, not niceness.

Jesus never calls us to compromise as a means to shine our light in the darkness. He alone can penetrate the darkness and he doesn't need us to manipulate circumstances for him. Our focus must always be on the light, intimately and humbly trusting him to reveal it through us.

## CREDIT GOD FOR OUR GOOD WORKS

We are not the light in order to legislate morality. That doesn't mean we can't be involved in politics, or that having legislation based on morality is unnecessary. In fact, the very nature of discipleship is that we take the life of Christ into the world. We cannot leave the life of Christ behind as we enter the marketplace or enter the political arena; we cannot compartmentalize our lives, segmenting Jesus to a portion of the weekend.

But we must always keep before us that our ability to be the light is not based upon civil law or legislative power. It is based upon the Son of God, the Morningstar, shining through us so that he can draw everyone to himself. We become people of the Light by believing in the Light and it is only through the Light that fallen man will see where he is going (John 12:27-36).

We are not even the light so we can set a good example. We are the light because our spirits have been illuminated by the extraordinary, piercing Light of the Cross. That light has its own agenda, and our duty is simply to obey the command of the one who is the Light of the World.

In fact, Jesus says we are to let our light shine so that others can see our good works, but those good works are seen, not to show us to be good, but to bring praise to our Father in heaven. In other words, the light shines on our good works so that other people can see the power of God in our lives. Bonhoeffer says "these works are none other than those which the Lord Jesus himself has created in them by calling them to be the light of the world under the shadow of his cross." Paul wrote that we are "created in Christ Jesus to do good works, which God prepared in advance for us to do" (Ephesians 2:10 NIV).

Our good works do not generate the light. The Cross alone illuminates the good works. Our good works do not reveal God; Jesus simply said others will see our good works and glorify God as a result. What becomes visible, Bonhoeffer says, are "the cross and the works of the cross, the poverty and renunciation of the blessed in the beatitudes."

If our good works were the source of the light, that could only be because we are virtuous—and we are decidedly not virtuous. If our virtue was the light that shines into the darkness, then it is us who deserves the glory, not God.

But God alone deserves glory. If we clothe the naked or visit the imprisoned or feed the hungry, we don't deserve praise. If we are called before a tribunal and are punished for our faith in Christ, we deserve no glory. We are merely being the light Christ has made us to be; we are simply shining from the hilltop on which he has placed us.

God along deserves to be praised for the transformation that has occurred in our lives. Bonhoeffer says, "It is by *seeing* the cross and the community beneath it that men come to believe in God. But that is the light of the Resurrection."

The apostle Paul says we should boast in "nothing but the Cross of our Master, Jesus Christ. Because of that Cross, I have been crucified in relation to the world, set free from the stifling atmosphere of pleasing others and fitting into the little patterns that they dictate. Can't you see the central issue in all this? It is not what you and I do—submit to circumcision, reject circumcision. It is what *God* is doing, and he is creating something totally new, a free life! All who walk by this standard are the true Israel of God—his chosen people. Peace and mercy on them" (Galatians 6:14-16 MSG).

✦

### The Cost of Discipleship—
I must give up the illusion that I create my influence and visibility and trust that God engineers these things through Jesus, who lives in me.

### Fallen Thinking—
- My influence and visibility is a result of my own efforts or because of my own goodness.
- I will help God change people by forcing them to be as good as me.
- I created and/or deserve my visibility and influence. They are mine to use as I please.

- My influence and visibility are measured by numbers, fame, money, and power. By seeking those, I can be a witness for Jesus.

## Kingdom Thinking—

- My influence and visibility is a result of who lives in me, not because of what I do.
- The penetrating power of Christ alone (salt and light penetrate) is able to transform others.
- God puts me in the place of influence and visibility.
- I am merely a steward of these things, so it is important I get out of the way and let Jesus work through me.
- Only God can measure the significance of my influence and visibility. I may influence one person who will then influence the world. My focus is on following Jesus wherever he may lead.

## Your Choice?

You do not need to try harder to be salt or light. The life of Jesus working in you makes it a natural outflow of your life. Will you abide in your obedience to Jesus, so that you will be salt and light to the world? Or will you live faithlessly, that is, in such a way that you can live your life without trusting Jesus?

# 8

## Becoming Like Jesus in Righteousness

*"Of course the righteousness of the disciples can never be a personal achievement;*
*it is always a gift, which they received when they were called to follow him."*
DIETRICH BONHOEFFER

*Do not think that I have come to do away with the Law of Moses and the*
*teachings of the prophets. I have not come to do away with them, but to*
*make their teachings come true. Remember that as long as heaven and earth*
*last, not the least point nor the smallest detail of the Law will be done away*
*with—not until the end of all things. So then, whoever disobeys even the least*
*important of the commandments and teaches others to do the same, will be*
*least in the Kingdom of heaven. On the other hand, whoever obeys the Law*
*and teaches others to do the same, will be great in the Kingdom of heaven.*
*I tell you, then, that you will be able to enter the Kingdom of heaven only if*
*you are more faithful than the teachers of the Law and the Pharisees in doing*
*what God requires.*

MATTHEW 5:17-20

Jesus' Objective—*To teach us that the gift of righteousness*
*does not excuse us from righteous living.*

Jesus did not come to abolish the law—even though a great many of us believe just that.

We think that because Jesus died for our sins and we are now forgiven, we can live as we please. We can fall into the "just be nice" mentality and assume the law—the standards of holiness—no longer apply.

This devilish thinking leads to the cheapening of grace, where we try to assume all the privileges of being a disciple of Jesus with none of the responsibilities. By trying to claim grace without the demands of holiness, we are, again, trying to separate grace from truth—and that is impossible since both are present in Jesus, whose life flows through us.

Bonhoeffer says it's not surprising when disciples jump to the conclusion that the law has been abolished because Jesus "reversed all popular notions of right and wrong, and pronounced a blessing on all that was accounted worthless." He notes it led Marcion, an early church heretic, to accuse the Jews of tampering with the text of Scripture. Marcion altered the words of Jesus to say: "Think ye that I am come to fulfil the law and the prophets? I am not come to fulfil, but to destroy."

Bonhoeffer notes: "How tempting then to suppose that Jesus would give the old order its *coup de grace* by repealing the law of the old covenant, and pronounce his followers free to enjoy the liberty of the Son of God!"

But Jesus very clearly upholds the law. In fact, he vindicates the claims of the law, saying, "I have not come to do away with them, but to make their teachings come true." (Matthew 5:17). Jesus looks at the law with an eye toward the end of days.

He is on a mission to bring us back into community with the Father, to get us through the narrow gate into the kingdom of heaven, and his view of eternity keeps him focused on the unity of the law. He knows the whole law must be fulfilled; every jot and tittle of the Old Testament commandments must be followed.

But Jesus also refuses to let the Ten Commandments sit on a pedestal above other parts of the law. When he says the disciples must be "more faithful than the teachers of the Law and the Pharisees in doing what God requires," he isn't limiting that faithfulness to just the Big Ten we tend to follow while ignoring what we perceive to be the lesser laws. (Matthew 5:20)

The Word says, "You must be obedient to the whole Law or else be found disobedient to the whole of the Law." There is no middle ground. To echo the apostles, "How can anyone possibly do this? This is humanly impossible!"

But that is the very point. It cannot be done, which is why Paul called the law *a school of Christ*, where we learn that trying to earn or maintain righteousness is impossible and so, in our broken state, we come to Christ and declare our dependence on him (Galatians 3:21-19). We follow Jesus, abandoning all else, *including our obsession with the law*.

But, again, this doesn't mean the law has been abandoned. It means the law has been fulfilled by Jesus and when we enter the realm of costly grace, we satisfy the law because the life of Jesus, who fulfilled the law, is flowing through us.

The apostle Paul says the "law of the Spirit, which brings us life in union with Christ Jesus, [sets us] free from the law of sin and death. What the Law could not do, because human nature was weak, God did." He sent Jesus to fulfill the law, "so that the righteous demands of the Law might be fully satisfied in us who live according to the Spirit, and not according to human nature" (Romans 8:2-4).

The thing Jesus knew—and which we so readily ignore—is that if you want to live under the law, you have to apply every bit of the law or you are in violation of the law. The law is unified. It will not allow you to simply make a list of which laws you think are important and which laws are insignificant. This picking and choosing is a form of legalism. We make our legal lists and they make us legalists.

And legalism does not require faith. In fact, legalism undermines our ability to develop an obedient trust in Jesus because it insists that we live by what we can see and touch. We have to see it to believe it; the exact opposite of we must believe it to see it, that is, those who are obedient will develop trust.

The apostle Paul says, "Rule-keeping does not naturally evolve into living by faith, but only perpetuates itself in more and more rule-keeping, a fact observed in Scripture: 'The one who does these things [rule-keeping]continues to live by them.' Christ redeemed us from that self-defeating, cursed life by absorbing it completely into himself" (Galatians 3:12-13a MSG).

But the problem with lists is that you not only have to accomplish every thing on the list perfectly, but just having the list gives you a false sense of security. It causes you to lose sight of the other parts of the law—the smallest details—that you failed to place on the list.

But worst of all, we end up following our lists instead of following Jesus. Once again, we can find ourselves moving quickly away from an intimate relationship with the Son. The apostle Paul says, "No one can sustain a relationship with God [this] way. The person who lives in right relationship with God does it by embracing what God arranges for him. Doing things for God is the opposite of entering into what God does for you. Habakkuk had it right: "The person who believes God, is set right by God—and that's the real life" (Galatians 3:11 MSG).

We are set right by God and not the rules we keep, but we are set right by our intimate relationship with Jesus, where we step into the costly grace he offers us. Trust and grace, again, are inseparable.

So when Jesus says he requires from us a more faithful pursuit of the law, he doesn't mean at all that we are capable of fulfilling every jot and tittle ourselves. Rather, he means we must live by faith in him, not by lists. We must live not by an independence born of cheap grace, but by obedience (which leads to belief) in him.

It is quite possible, notes Bonhoeffer, to adhere to the law religiously and not be a follower of Jesus Christ because discipleship means we adhere to Jesus Christ alone, Jesus is the manifestation of the law in "perfect union with the will of God as revealed in the Old Testament law and prophets," Bonhoeffer says. When we follow Jesus, we enter into that unique union with Jesus that allows us to share in the righteousness better than the Pharisees.

## GRACE AND OBEDIENCE ARE INSEPARABLE

Speaking of Jesus, Bonhoeffer says, "He has in fact nothing to add to the commandments of God, except this, that he keeps them. He fulfils the law, and he tells us so himself, therefore it must be true. . . . But that means that he must die, he alone understands the true nature of the law as God's law: the law is not itself God, nor is God the law. It was the error of Israel to put the law in God's place, to make the law their God and their God a law."

On the other hand, Bonhoeffer says the temptation of the disciples was to imagine that the law could be separated from God. He says, in both cases, God is equally denied. We deny God when we elevate the law above grace—making the law an idol, worshipping the law as idolaters. And we deny God when we claim the promise of salvation through faith in Jesus while not taking responsibility for holy living.

How can we imagine for a moment that we could claim holiness while living devilishly? Yet that is precisely what we do when we remain submerged in fallen thinking and, therefore, fallen living instead of actively pursuing the holiness demanded by the costly grace of Jesus.

Grace in no way frees us from the pursuit of holiness. In truth, grace is given to us to make it holy living possible. Imagine holy living as a high wire that you must walk across. One slip and you tumble, forever lost, into the chasm below. But now Jesus stretches a safety net across the chasm. When you slip, you fall into the safety net of grace, acknowledge your mistake, and climb back on the high wire—all the while with Jesus helping and supporting you.

Walking across the chasm on the high wire is now a perfectly reasonable request. If you try to walk across but you're constantly afraid of slipping, then you deny the grace of Jesus—and you are living like a legalist.

On the other hand, if you try to walk across but you have a cavalier attitude about your steps, even doing things that cause you to fall off the high wire, then you've embraced the concept of cheap grace.

But what Jesus provides is a net of costly grace. He will keep us from falling forever into the chasm, but we must follow him and take the steps he teaches us to take. Grace and obedience are not two separate issues; they are inseparably bound together in such a way that you cannot claim to be under grace while demanding freedom from obedience.

## OBEY THE LAW AND TEACH OTHERS TO DO THE SAME

Bonhoeffer says the Pharisees knew that the law must be obeyed: "Their ideal was to model their behavior exactly on the demands of the law." But they knew it couldn't be done and so they focused on the nuances of the law, and this allowed them to claim the law was being fulfilled. In a sense, they created a religious system where the law was the ideal, but keeping certain rules was the best they could do. It allowed them to feel good about themselves when they were, in reality, lowering the standards of the law. They became masters at observing the letter of the law, while ignoring its spirit.

Bonhoeffer says the Pharisees remind us "that it is possible to teach the law without fulfilling it, to teach it in such a way that it cannot be fulfilled." He adds: "That sort of teaching has no warrant from Jesus. The law will be obeyed as certainly as he obeyed it himself. If men cleave to him who fulfilled the law and follow him, they will find themselves both teaching and fulfilling the law. Only the doer of the law can remain in communion with Jesus."

We must move from merely being teachers of the word to being doers of the word, notes Bonhoeffer. We no longer just study the word; we become it. As we submit ourselves to the Word that lives within us, we are transformed, by grace, and conformed to his image.

By virtue of our union with Christ in us, we are what we could never otherwise become. We become righteous because—and only because—the one in whom we abide is the very incarnation of holiness.

This is real righteousness—true holiness—because we are one with holy Christ and we obey our Lord when he commands. Then, as Romans 12:2 says, we no longer are conformed to this world, but transformed by the renewing of our minds—and able to "prove what the will of God is, that which is good and acceptable and perfect" (NAS).

When we are in union with Christ and obey his commands, we do the will of God and fulfill the law of God. We transcend the teaching of the law, and become doers of the law of Christ. "This is where the righteousness of the disciple exceeds that of the Pharisees," says Bonhoeffer. "It is grounded solely upon the call to fellowship with him who alone fulfils the law."

❧

### The Cost of Discipleship—

Our righteousness flows from the life of Jesus into us. We must obediently trust this is true and stop trying harder to be holy. By trusting more, we will become obedient to the commands of Jesus.

### Fallen Thinking—

- God's grace allows me to live however I please.
- It's okay for me to sin because Jesus has to forgive me.
- I must get to know all of the "to do" lists so I can be holy.
- I live a righteous life and that makes me righteous.
- Grace is separate from obedience; if I have grace I don't need obedience.

**Kingdom Thinking—**

- I live holy because I trust Jesus and obey his commands.
- I will keep myself from sin, but if I stumble, I trust Jesus will forgive me.
- I am holy righteous because the holy righteous One lives in me.
- I will never find peace or joy in unholy, unrighteous behaviors.
- I may at anytime live from the holy righteous life of Christ by abiding in him and abandoning to him.
- Jesus Christ is my standard for holiness and righteousness; I do not compare contrast myself to others.
- Grace and obedience are inseparable.

**Your Choice?**

Will I trust the righteousness of Jesus in me? Or, will I try harder to earn my way into heaven?

# 9

# BECOMING LIKE JESUS IN AUTHENTICITY

*"Not just the fact that I am angry, but the fact that there is
somebody who has been hurt, damaged and disgraced by me, who
"has a cause against me," erects a barrier between me and God."*

DIETRICH BONHOEFFER

*You have heard that people were told in the past, 'Do not commit murder;
anyone who does will be brought to trial.' But now I tell you: if you are angry
with your brother you will be brought to trial, if you call your brother 'You
good-for-nothing!' you will be brought before the Council, and if you call your
brother a worthless fool you will be in danger of going to the fire of hell.*

*So if you are about to offer your gift to God at the altar and there you
remember that your brother has something against you, leave your gift there
in front of the altar, go at once and make peace with your brother, and then
come back and offer your gift to God.*

*If someone brings a lawsuit against you and takes you to court, settle the
dispute while there is time, before you get to court. Once you are there, you will
be turned over to the judge, who will hand you over to the police, and you will
be put in jail. There you will stay, I tell you, until you pay the last penny of
your fine.*

MATTHEW 5:21-26

Jesus' Objective—*To teach us that life flows from God through Jesus into us
and so our authenticity is measured in our hearts and not by our appearances.*

God never intended for us to live under the law; he designed us to live in
communion with him. Because our sin broke that communion, God gave
us the law, starting with the Ten Commandments, to push us toward holy living.

But the law was never meant to be the means for bringing us back to community with God. . The apostle Paul says it was meant to be a school of Christ that would teach us not only the holy ways of God but also the impossibility of meeting those standards apart from divine help. God gave us the law so we would realize how much we need him; so we could learn just how *dependent* we are upon his grace to get us back to where we now belong.

Jesus calls us to follow him into an extraordinary life, a life spent in pursuit of the things that matter to him; a life lived inside the borders of the kingdom of heaven.

Jesus offers no compromise to those who insist on following the law instead of him. He makes it clear that the law demands perfection and, if that isn't enough to topple our arrogance, he explains how perfection is interpreted in the kingdom of heaven. The law says do not commit murder, but understand that includes character assassination. If you've so much as whispered an insult against another person, then you have committed murder. You have already lost your chance to earn your way into the kingdom of heaven.

Most people would assume they can at least make the cut when it comes to murder. *I mean, at least I haven't murdered anyone.* But Jesus knows "The tongue has the power of life and death . . ." (Proverbs 18:21a NIV) and so, as Bonhoeffer notes, he declares anger to be an attack on another's life with an aim of destruction. "The angry word is a blow struck at our brother, a stab at his heart: it seeks to hit, to hurt and to destroy," says Bonhoeffer.

Jesus says the motivations of the heart are more important than appearance. When our motive is to hurt, destroy, or exclude others, we share the same motive with one who murders.

"A deliberate insult is even worse," Bonhoeffer adds, "for we are then openly disgracing our brother in the eyes of the world, and causing others to despise him. With our hearts burning with hatred, we seek to annihilate his moral and material existence. We are passing judgment on him, and that is murder. And the murderer will himself be judged."

He declares that the slammed door; the if-looks-could-kill stare; the menacing tone; the threatening language; the cold shoulder; the pointed finger; the phrase that blames are all acts of murder against God's creations; those who have been created by God as eternal beings; those who carry sin and shortcomings no different than the disciples of Jesus. *There but for the grace of God go I.*

There's no way you could ever meet God's standard, but the good news is you don't have to because Jesus covers your sins, allowing you to become intimate with God. This freedom, in Christ, means you can be who you were meant to be and live how you were meant to live. Love God and live accordingly!

## KINGDOM HEARTS, KINGDOM THINKING

Jesus, again, pushes the disciples toward kingdom thinking, where racist slurs and degrading terms are all instruments of murder and no different than the blast of a shotgun into the face of our adversary.

We use such terms to dehumanize those who oppose us, who are different from us, who don't agree with us, who are a danger to us. We live in a fallen world—Jesus is well aware of that—and so it would be naive to assume we will not run up against real evil that is out to destroy us, but the point is that even those engaged in evil are God's creatures, living with a fallen nature, no different than you and I before Jesus breathed life into our dead spirit.

Kingdom thinking requires that we stop seeing other people, even our enemies, as people we can degrade or judge. Just like us, they are beings in need of God's grace. "There but for the grace of God go I" is a legitimate consideration as we interact with friends and foes alike.

Again, as C. S. Lewis explains in *Mere Christianity*, we're all eternal beings. The question that remains to be answered is where each of us will spend eternity: in the kingdom of heaven or in the dominion of hell.

And perhaps the point that needs to linger with us is that we murder—commit character assassination—far more people who annoy us than against any real enemy to our health and well-being. Most of us feel pretty confident that murder is the one law we will never break and that may be the very reason Jesus used it as an example to show that it is humanly impossible to be perfect under the law.

God's redemptive plan includes the chance for our enemies—and even those who merely annoy us—to come into the kingdom of God under the righteousness of Jesus Christ. They enter in the same way we enter the kingdom

of heaven—despite our sins, despite our own weaknesses and imperfections;
despite the evil we have done against others.

## DIVIDED HEARTS, DIVIDED WORSHIP

And because Jesus wants to redeem even our enemies, he cannot allow us to
worship with divided hearts, where we claim to love God while we are in really
conflict with another believer. Jesus is as interested in your enemy's salvation as
he is in yours and he wants your interest in your enemy's salvation as well. To
echo Rick Warren, from *The Purpose Driven Life*, the disciples of Jesus must care
about the things Jesus cares about.

Bonhoeffer says no matter how correct our liturgy, no matter how devout our
prayer, no matter how brave our testimony, they will profit us nothing and, in
truth, will even testify against us, if we do not love other believers enough to
make things right with them. God "wants no honour for himself so long as our
brother is dishonoured," says Bonhoeffer.

Jesus will not allow us to separate our worship of God from our service to
others. They are one in the same, just as Jesus worshiped God by his sacrificial
service toward us. "God is the Father, the Father of our Lord Jesus Christ, who
became the Brother of us all," says Bonhoeffer. ". . . The Father would not be
separated from his Son, nor will he now turn his face from those whose likeness
the Son took upon him, and for whose sake he bore the shame. The Incarnation
is the ultimate reason why the service of God cannot be divorced from the service of man. He who says he loves God and hates his brother is a liar."

When we worship together, we become the instruction manual of heaven's reality. We show our oneness with God's glory and our unity with other believers,
praising God with our hearts as one. We're to intentionally remove any obstacles
to our unity with other believers so that with "one heart and mouth [we] may
glorify the God and Father of our Lord Jesus Christ" (Romans 15:6 NIV).

Jesus considered our unity with one another so critical that he said we should
stop worship and go set things right with anyone who is at odds with us. "Then
and only then, come back and work things out with God" (Matthew 5:23-24
MSG). What if we agreed not to have worship services until everyone in the
congregation set things right with each other? How quickly would conflicts
be resolved?

Another thing Jesus is getting at is that we cannot pretend to be one thing when we are something else. Doing this disconnects us from reality but, worse, it gets us in the habit of separating who we are from what we pretend we are—or what we think we are. This devilish dichotomy undermines our journey into the kingdom of heaven. It leaves us stuck at a point of immaturity even though Jesus calls us to engage the new life God has put within, a life that will bring us into authentic Christian maturity.

✑

### The Cost of Discipleship—

I can no longer allow my heart to be counter to the character of Christ. I must be authentic in the way I live, keeping my actions in line with heart and my heart in line with Jesus.

### Fallen Thinking—

- I can hide what is in my heart, even from God.
- If people see what is in my heart, they won't love me.
- If I try harder, I can change my heart to conform to Jesus.
- I do not feel loving toward _____, so I cannot really love her/him.
- He's lucky I don't get to decide his punishment,
- Even God couldn't straighten her out.
- I can't sit next to him in the worship service; I don't even like him!

### Kingdom Thinking—

- God sees and knows all of me and loves me anyway (Hebrews 4:13)
- When I obediently trust Jesus, my heart will conform to his.
- God comes and search my heart for I know you are love and always have my best interest in mind. My feelings and thoughts may mislead me but God will not.
- Jesus, the way I am acting is not in line with your character. Show me the part of my heart that is still independent from you.

- My unwillingness to reconcile with my brother is really my insistence on remaining independent from Jesus.
- I do not feel loving toward _____, but Jesus can love her/him through me. My love is not based on my feelings; it is based on the life of Christ flowing through me.
- God loved me even while I was still his enemy; He is teaching me to love others, even if they do not love me.

## Your Choice?

The cost of pretense is always higher that the cost of discipleship. Every time we pretend, something dies (Acts 5). In trusting and obeying, we allow real life to flow through us. Will you live in the reality of life as it is found in Jesus, or will you pretend life can be lived independent of him? (Colossians 3)

# 10

## Becoming Like Jesus in Purity

*"To follow Jesus means self-renunciation and absolute adherence to him, and therefore a will dominated by lust can never be allowed to do what it likes."*

DIETRICH BONHOEFFER

*You have heard that it was said, 'Do not commit adultery.' But now I tell you: anyone who looks at a woman and wants to possess her is guilty of committing adultery with her in his heart.*

*So if your right eye causes you to sin, take it out and throw it away! It is much better for you to lose a part of your body than to have your whole body thrown into hell.*

*If your right hand causes you to sin, cut it off and throw it away! It is much better for you to lose one of your limbs than to have your whole body go off to hell.*

*"It was also said, 'Anyone who divorces his wife must give her a written notice of divorce.' But now I tell you: if a man divorces his wife for any cause other than her unfaithfulness, then he is guilty of making her commit adultery if she marries again; and the man who marries her commits adultery also.*

MATTHEW 5:27-32

Jesus' Objective—*To teach the disciples that lust is impure because it is unbelief, and therefore it is to be shunned.*

Lust shows a lack of faith. We sell "our heavenly birthright for a mess of pottage," says Bonhoeffer, trading off the promises of God for something startlingly insignificant. "The gains of lust are trivial compared with the loss it brings—you forfeit your body eternally for the momentary pleasure of eye or hand," says Bonhoeffer.

The only appropriate place to give our desires free rein is within the context of godly love, where we look to the best interests of others and where we see each individual as a child of God, created to carry the Christ-Spirit.

Lust reveals we're distant from Jesus. Consider how hard it is to lust after someone while holding Christ in your thoughts. Try praying for the one you lust for and see how quickly the prayer or the lust wins out: one or the other because you cannot serve two masters. "When you have made your eye the instrument of impurity, you cannot see God with it," says Bonhoeffer.

Yet, Bonhoeffer notes, Jesus is not unreasonable or impractical in his prohibitions. He doesn't forbid them from looking at anything; rather, he says his disciples should look to him. "If they do that he knows that their gaze will always be pure, even when they look upon a woman."

Jesus cites infidelity as justification for divorce, but his point is you haven't "preserved your virtue simply by staying out of bed. Your *heart* can be corrupted by lust even quicker than your *body*. Those leering looks you think nobody notices—they also corrupt" (Matthew 5:28 MSG).

While affirming the Old Testament law, Jesus declares righteousness is at a higher level than we could ever hope to attain. Jesus' standard renders every one of us guilty of adultery. "Man does not see what the Lord sees, for man sees what is visible, but the Lord sees the heart" (1 Samuel 16:7b HCSB).

Jesus isn't on mission to support a religion of appearances; he requires we be pure from the inside out. And he says, *"Let's not pretend this is easier than it really is. If you want to live a morally pure life, here's what you have to do: You have to blind your right eye the moment you catch it in a lustful leer. You have to choose to live one-eyed or else be dumped on a moral trash pile. And you have to chop off your right hand the moment you notice it raised threateningly. Better a bloody stump than your entire being discarded for good in the dump"* (Matthew 5:29-30 MSG).

## IT TAKES FAITH TO BE FAITHFUL

Jesus knows you're fighting against natural instincts and he's not insensitive to your plight. He was human; he struggled with the same temptations you do. Is he telling you to get tough and defeat this lust issue on your own?

Actually, no. He knows you can't do it on your own. Instead of fighting against your basic instincts, Jesus wants you to step into his grace. The costly grace Jesus died to give you a free gift. Jesus went to the cross to pay for your sin of lust, but he rose from the dead to give you new life, a new way to confront the sin of lust.

Jesus wants to replace your instinct with the Holy Spirit so that, instead of being a slave to impulse, you are free to make pure choices when it comes to lust and sex. Through the Holy Spirit, you have the power of the divine nature working inside you. You access that power through faith—believing the Spirit is there and at work to help you overcome the sin of lust.

When you are tempted, you have a choice: do you believe fulfilling your lust is best for you or do you believe that the reason Jesus condemns lust is because he knows it will keep you from becoming all that you can be. Believe Jesus or believe your impulses?

The Apostle Paul says, *"It is God's will that you should be sanctified: that you should avoid sexual immorality; that each of you should learn to control his own body in a way that is holy and honorable, not in passionate lust like the heathen, who do not know God . . . For God did not call us to be impure, but to live a holy life.*

*Therefore, he who rejects this instruction does not reject man but God, who gives you his Holy Spirit"* (1 Thessalonians 4:3-5, 7-8 NIV, italics added).

The disciple's life is more than growing in spiritual maturity; even our bodies figure into discipleship. The apostle Paul pleads with the believers in Romans to offer their very bodies to Christ (Romans 12:1) and points out to the Corinthian church that they ought to glorify God in their bodies because "you are not your own"—we have been bought with a price. God's Son took on a human body and it was crucified; we are part of his body and also must be crucified. "And those who belong to Christ Jesus have put to death their human nature with all its passions and desires. The Spirit has given us life; he must also control our lives" (Galatians 5:25-26).

"Lust is impure because it is unbelief, and therefore it is to be shunned," says Bonhoeffer. It requires faith to be faithful. "[Jesus] liberates marriage from selfish, evil desire, and consecrates it to the service of love, which is possible only in a life of discipleship."

**The Cost of Discipleship—**

"The body is not to be used for sexual immorality, but to serve the Lord; and the Lord provides for the body" (1 Corinthians 6:13b).

**Fallen Thinking—**
- Since my spirit is where Christ dwells, what happens in my body doesn't really matter.

**Kingdom Thinking—**
- Anything that morally or spiritually traps-- that causes me to fall into sin or to stay in sin—should be eliminated quickly and totally.
- To avoid impurity, I must be conscious and purposeful about what is around me, where I go, what I do, what I watch and read, and the conversations I have.
- Yet, the solution to sexual impurity cannot be external because the cause is not just external.
- The body is more than biological, as divine judgment will reveal: "Don't you know that your body is the temple of the Holy Spirit, who lives in you and who was given to you by God? You do not belong to yourselves but to God; he bought you for a price. So use your bodies for God's glory." (1 Corinthians 6:19-20

**You Choice?**

Will I be compelled by love or driven by lust?

# 11

## Becoming Like Jesus in Transparency

*"Complete truthfulness is only possible where sin has been uncovered, and forgiven by Jesus. Only those who are in a state of truthfulness through the confession of their sin to Jesus are not ashamed to tell the truth wherever it must be told."*

Dietrich Bonhoeffer

*You have also heard that people were told in the past, 'Do not break your promise, but do what you have vowed to the Lord to do.' But now I tell you: do not use any vow when you make a promise. Do not swear by heaven, for it is God's throne; nor by earth, for it is the resting place for his feet; nor by Jerusalem, for it is the city of the great King. Do not even swear by your head, because you cannot make a single hair white or black. Just say 'Yes' or 'No'—anything else you say comes from the Evil One.*

Matthew 5:33-37

Jesus' Objective—*To teach us that our ability to be honest in all situations is a reflection of how much we trust Jesus.*

Jesus commands you to follow the truth no matter where it leads. This means you live the truth and speak the truth at all times. It is impossible to follow truth and also following a lie. It's like trying to hold onto two lovers at once; your desire to please one will leave you feeling contempt for the other (Matthew 6:24 MSG). You will either love the truth or you will love the lie, but you cannot love them both.

You must make a choice: Will you follow the truth or will you follow the lie?

Jesus told the self-righteous they were children of the Devil, who is the father of lies (John 8:44). You cannot be a child of the truth and remain a child of the lie. Jesus leaves no middle ground: you belong to the truth or you belong to the lie.

We may think we're obeying the truth by condemning the lies of others, but Jesus won't allow us to use their lies to distract us from our own. If we listen, we can hear him say, "The one who has never lied may throw the first stone."

There's only one way to obey this commandment from Jesus and that is to drop the stones we hold. We're not qualified to condemn others. The only one qualified to throw the first stone is Jesus, and his choice is to forgive. He says, "I do not condemn you either. Go, but do not sin again" (John 3:18 NIV).

This grace is a gift from God, but the cost of grace is that we let Jesus change our lives so that we live and breath and speak the truth. Jesus doesn't say, "You're forgiven; now you can go back to living a lie."

## WHEN YOU LIE, YOU OPPOSE JESUS

Jesus is the Truth. When you lie, you declare that you're against Jesus. Hypocrisy—living a lie—is an assault upon Jesus. Self-righteousness declares that Jesus is a liar because it says something—"self"—must be added to his righteousness.

The self-righteous attacked Jesus because of his friendship with sinners. Were they suggesting, if Jesus were friends with them, he would no longer be associated with sinners? Weren't they sinners, too? Or, were they somehow excluded from the list of *all* have sinned.

But Jesus will not allow that; when Truth speaks, the sinner is you: "For all have sinned and fall short of the glory of God" (Romans 3:23 NIV).

And here, then, is a mystery, for the sinners surrounding Jesus are closer to the Truth than the self-righteous who stand apart and throw stones. Like people in recovery, the friends of Jesus are willing to become intimate with the Truth, even though they know it will expose their lies. They've come to intimately trust there is no where else to go, except to follow the Truth, and so they're ready to abandon the foolish fantasy that they can still be loyal to a lie while loving the Truth.

They are, as Jesus said, people who need a doctor, but they also know they need a doctor and that is what separates them from those who use lies, manipulation, and hypocrisy to keep up the appearance that they have a healthy, intimate relationship with truth. You cannot lie to the Truth.

Jesus calls us and he reveals himself to us. We do not call him and we cannot control the things about ourselves that we reveal to him. He knows about our sins. There is nothing that can be hidden from him. Every dark and dangerous thing about us is uncovered when we enter into fellowship with Jesus, when we enter into the realm of truth. Yet, Jesus still calls us.

Think of it like this: If we were calling Jesus to our turf, we could control where the meeting takes place. We could limit what Jesus sees. We could set the stage so he'd walk through a specific door and sit in a specific seat and he'd never be able to see where we've stuffed our sin. We could pull off the appearance of godliness while keeping our devilish thoughts and behaviors hidden from his sight.

But Jesus calls us to his turf. We can't control the circumstances of the call; all we can do is respond. There's no place to hide when we walk into the white light of the incarnate truth (Matthew 17:2). We enter on his terms and the last thing the Truth wants is for us to hide our sins. He wants them all out in the open so we can see them in light of the truth; no longer hidden beneath shadows that suggest our sins aren't so bad.

Jesus wants to reveal them all, so that, against the purity of his truth, we finally see that God's standard of truth is so high—so perfect—that it is humanly impossible to reach. Only then will we come to the place where we understand our need for redemption, where, like the apostle Paul, we see we've come to the end of our rope: "What an unhappy man I am! Who will rescue me from this body that is taking me to death" (Romans 7:24).

We no longer want the lie within us; we no longer want to live a life of lies. We believe in God's Truth, and we believe the Truth can set us free: "What you're after is truth from the inside out. Enter me, then; conceive a new, true life. Remove my sin, and I will be clean; wash me, and I will be whiter than snow" (Psalms 51:6-7).

## OUR DESPAIR PREPARES US FOR GRACE

Despite his impeccable integrity, the prophet Isaiah was overwhelmed with the unholiness of his life when brought before the Truth. He saw his need for grace and cried, "There is no hope for me! I am doomed because every word that passes my lips is sinful, and I live among a people whose every word is sinful" (Isaiah 6:5).

Perhaps it was in this moment that Isaiah understood that even our greatest acts of righteousness and our most honest behaviors are like filthy rags when compared to God's holy standards (Isaiah 64:6).

Yet, Isaiah's story shows that Jesus never intends to leave us in despair (Romans 7:24-25 MSG). His intent is to prepare us to receive God's grace. Even as Isaiah is staggered by the revelation of his sin, Isaiah just as suddenly finds himself cleansed of his guilt and forgiven of his sins when he is touched by a burning coal from heaven's altar (Isaiah 6:7). He is then energized for God's purpose: "Then I heard the Lord say, "Whom shall I send? Who will be our messenger?" I answered, "I will go! Send me" (Isaiah 6:8).

In the same way, our call to discipleship cleanses us and energizes us to follow Jesus. But we have to face the truth about ourselves, or the lie will constantly undermine our ability to follow Jesus.

Truthfulness requires complete transparency. Every corner of our soul must be exposed by Jesus; all the evil in our being must be laid bare. We humans not only resist such truth-telling, we persecute and crucify it. It is only because Jesus lives in us that we are able to live in authentic, transparent truthfulness. "The cross is God's truth about us, and therefore it is the only power which can make us truthful," Bonhoeffer says. "When we know the cross, we are no longer afraid of the truth."

The cross is God's truth about us and anything we do to side step this truth simply leaves us in a lie. If we could reach God's standard of truth on our own, if we could fulfill the requirements of the law, then Christ died for nothing (Galatians 2:21 paraphrase). Our self-righteousness is nothing less than an arrogant assault upon the holiness of God and when we wink at our sin—any sin—we cheapen the bloody price that Jesus paid to cleanse us from those sins.

## TRUTH CREATES AUTHENTICITY WITHIN COMMUNITY

If we can't get honest before Jesus, then we'll find it difficult to get honest in our congregations. We'll find people crucifying the Truth because they're unwilling to crucify the self, living by lists that nurture the lie they're living up to the law.

We'll find others who sacrifice the truth because they think that grace is all about getting along and going along.

The fact is we cannot have true, authentic, Christian community without truth because our relationship with Jesus, the Truth, effects the truthfulness and transparency of our relationship with all others.

It is only in this transparent community that we can see each other as we truly are, where we can grow up in Christ, speaking the truth in love as iron sharpens iron. In such a truth community, there is no need to "read between the lines or look for hidden meanings" because we speak "a plain, unembellished truth . . ." (2 Corinthians 1:13 MSG). We need not fear exposure because everything is already out in the open and everyone in the community is committed to speaking the truth, living the truth, and following the truth no matter where it leads.

"We refuse to wear masks and play games. We don't maneuver and manipulate behind the scenes. And we don't twist God's Word to suit ourselves. Rather, we keep everything we do and say out in the open, the whole truth on display, so that those who want to can see and judge for themselves in the presence of God" (2 Corinthians 4:2 MSG).

A utopia? Certainly not by the standards of Jesus, the Truth Incarnate.

Impossible? Absolutely, if we try to create such a community independent of the Truth incarnate.

And this is our constant challenge: Will we try to define truth separate from God's standard? Will we try to live independent of the one who is the Truth? Will we compromise on the truth, or try to waste our efforts trying to reach a compromise with the Truth Incarnate? Will we ignore the Truth and live a lie?

We cannot answer these questions once and consider the matter settled. We answer them throughout the day, every day, as we make decisions, both large and small, regarding how far we will follow the Truth.

And this leads to the matter of making oaths.

Oaths are a mechanism to verify that we are telling the truth or that we will keep our promise. But Jesus calls us to be so reliable in telling the truth that others will always know what we say is true simply because it is our word. Our "yes means yes" and our "no means no."

The promise is in our word, not within an oath. We are in union with the Truth and those around us can trust that we will always be truthful in life, truthful in action, and truthful in speech. Jesus is the Truth and we are becoming like Jesus.

Consider it this way: We don't need to swear on the Bible, God's Word, because the Word of God lives in our hearts. We are living, breathing extensions of the Truth, telling the truth—"so help me God"—because the Truth of God is truly helping us tell the truth.

In addition, Bonhoeffer notes we can only commit to the future with the sense of God willing because we not only do not know what the future holds, we never want to end up in a situation where our oath takes precedence over our allegiance to Jesus. A disciple of Jesus is bound to the will of God alone.

This doesn't mean giving an oath is wrong. God allows them. The Bible says they are to be voluntary promises, given only after seriously counting the costs of the promise. And, once we make an oath, the Bible says we should be very deliberate in fulfilling our promise (Deuteronomy 23:21-23).

The problem Jesus had with oaths is that, when used with an improper motive, they can corrupt or manipulate the truth. In essence, they create a hierarchy of honesty, where under oath we swear to tell the whole truth and nothing but the truth, but when we're not under oath, we have the ability to say whatever we want regarding the truth.

The result is a systematic downgrading of truth, where it's not only accepted, but expected, that people will not be completely honest or keep their promises. And, like frogs in a kettle, we never notice when the dishonesty moves from lukewarm lies to a boiling hot hypocrisy, creating a double-standard for truth that pervades our relationships and our culture.

We take it for granted today that there's a hierarchy of honesty, where we can say anything we want off-the-record, yet cautiously measure our words when we're on-the-record. It's the way we justify plausible deniability, where our claim to have no knowledge of wrong-doing is correct, not because our claim is the truth, but because a carefully constructed lie allows us to say it is technically true.

Even when we take an oath, there is no guarantee that we're telling the truth. If I'm called to court and placed under oath, it's accepted, if not expected, that I am within my rights to limit how much of the truth I will reveal. My attorney will most likely instruct me to give precise answers to specific questions and to not volunteer any information that does not benefit my case. The emphasis is on the legal obligation to tell the truth, not the moral obligation to reveal the whole truth.

With divine tenacity, Jesus faced off against this hypocrisy. Once again, the self-righteous were focused on outside behavior. They were teaching people to verify the truth through an oath with little regard as to whether the oath really reflected the truth. "On the outside you appear to people as righteous," Jesus later said. "But on the inside you are full of hypocrisy and wickedness" (Matthew 23:28 NIV).

## OATHS CREATE A CHRISTLESS SYSTEM

And these were God's shepherds, responsible for pointing others to the Truth. They knew full well it was humanly impossible to meet the demands of the law, even when it came to telling the truth. Yet, instead of seeking God's provision for meeting the demands of the law—Jesus, the Truth from the Father—they created a set of rules that excused disobedience to God's law. Oaths were being used as the smoke and mirror to hide the fact that the self-righteous shepherds were lowering the requirements for righteousness.

Jesus, who was always aware of the big picture, knew that even a little lie is an assault upon the holiness of God and an attempt to undermine his sovereignty. We try to make it a little thing by focusing on the smallness of the behavior, but Jesus cannot allow us to ignore the enormity of any lie when measured against kingdom standards.

His gaze remains vigilant to the end-game, where "whoever believes in him is not condemned, but whoever does not believe stands condemned already because he has not believed in the name of God's one and only Son" (John 3:18 NIV). Jesus was on a mission to bring us into the kingdom under the King's grace (John 3:16-21).

Is it any wonder, then, that Jesus challenged such a Christless system, where man's rules were established above God's law, where the truth was declared independent of God's incarnate Truth? Why do we need Jesus if we can satisfy God's standards for truth through our own efforts?

The only way to lower the standards for truth is to make them independent of Jesus, the Truth incarnate. And when we do that, the truth is an unprotected orphan, dependent upon the situation or self-interest. Truth becomes relative and we become cynical about the truth. When someone swears the check is in the mail, we doubt it is even been written. When he swears on his grandmother's grave that he will pay by Thursday, we're certain he's not sincere. When he swears on a stack of Bibles that what he is saying is true, do we finally believe him?

Like Pilate, like the age we live in, we ask, "What is truth?" We doubt there really is an answer. It depends on all sorts of thing—because it does not depend on the Truth Incarnate.

The real issue is this: if your word can't be trusted, then even an oath won't guarantee you're telling the truth. So Jesus says, instead of all these declarations of truthfulness, wouldn't it be better to just tell the truth all the time—that way people will know you are being honest every time you opened your mouth. And they'll know you'll always do what you promise to do? Just let your "yes" mean "yes" and your "no" mean "no?"

What does this mean?

**Say only what you mean**—"When you manipulate words to get your own way, you go wrong" (Matthew 5:37 MSG; see also James 5:12).

**Say only what is true**—When we lie, we speak in the Devil's "native language," for he is a liar (John 8:44 NIV). It doesn't matter if the lie is black or white, a little fib or an outrageous whopper. In the kingdom of heaven, obedience to the King means we no longer lie to others; we no longer lie to ourselves; and we no longer lie to God.

**Don't imply that something is true when it isn't**—Many people would never consider telling an outright lie; yet, they habitually tell lies of omission. This happens when they leave critical information out of a conversation in order to deliberately leave a false impression. For instance, your boss compliments you on a job well done and you fail to let him know that a colleague actually did the work.

**Hypocrisy is just another way to lie**—When we maneuver and manipulate, twist and hide, pretend and posture, we're engaged in lies without words.

Bonhoeffer notes, "We need no more oaths to confirm the truth of our utterances, for we live in the perfect truth of God." And because we live and breathe and have our being in God's Truth, the reality for a disciple is this:

When we hide the truth, it is a faith issue, not a circumstance issue.

It takes faith to be truthful. It takes faith to come clean. It takes faith to be authentic and transparent in our relationships. It takes faith to stop pretending and to let others see who we really are and what we're really about.

Praise God, we have Jesus, our mediator. Even if we sin, we need not live in fear because he sits at the right hand of the Father as our advocate. He understands our weaknesses; he was tempted in "every way that we are, but did not sin. Let us have confidence, then, and approach God's throne, where there is grace. There we will receive mercy and find grace to help us just when we need it" (Hebrews 4:14-16).

The point is: Jesus wants to cleanse us; not condemn us. Jesus wants to do whatever is necessary to cleanse us of our sins so we can come home to the Father. Again and again, we see Jesus in the New Testament willing to use his power to heal; we see him willing to use his authority to cleanse.

If, while earth-bound, Jesus showed compassion for people in need, why would he be any different today? The difference is not with him; it is with the lie within us that whispers God sent his son into the world to condemn it, not to save—a contradiction of God's Word. The hiss of the serpent that says the yoke of Jesus is heavy and hard, and so we must hide from the Truth (John 3:17-18).

*"A man with a dreaded disease once came to Jesus and said, 'Sir, if you want to, you can make me clean.' Jesus reached out and touched him. 'I do want to,' he answered. 'Be clean!' At once the man was healed of his disease"* (Matthew 8:2-3). Today, Jesus still says, "I do want to."

He wants us to be with him in his kingdom (John 17:24). His whole mission was to "rescue us from the present evil age" (Galatians 1:4 NIV).

## IS IT EVER APPROPRIATE TO TELL A LIE?

There is one final question that should be asked when a disciple of Jesus considers truth. Is it ever appropriate to tell a lie? What if the lie is to spare someone's feelings—as in, "What do you think of my new hairstyle?" What if the lie is to save a life—such as if you were asked by a Nazi in 1940, "Tell me, Christian, are you hiding any Jews in your attic?"

There is a branch of Christian ethics that takes such questions and stacks them in priority, creating another hierarchy of truth, where a lie in order to save a life is clearly more acceptable than telling a lie for personal gain.[8] But Bonhoeffer would argue that any such debate simply distracts us from Jesus.

The issue is not whether a particular lie is more forgivable, the issue is that we need to be forgiven. A lie is a lie, and a lie is sin, and that brings us short of God's standards.

Listen carefully on this: Our arguments are to make the lie acceptable and we've long established that we cannot clean up our sin, even the little white lie that we tell. But we're looking the wrong way and that is exactly Bonhoeffer's point. When we look to Jesus, we see that our sins are forgiven, so stop arguing about the acceptability of any form of lie. Just fall on the grace of Jesus.

Does that give us a license to lie? As the apostle Paul would say, *God forbid it* (Romans 6:1-2). Of course not, but it does mean we have freedom in Christ to maneuver through the murky moments of life and know that God is still on our side if we fail to be perfect. When we fear making mistakes, we become trapped in *anti-faith* lives, afraid to move with the bold confidence God's grace gives us to walk in times of uncertainty (Hebrews 10:19–25).

But the privilege of walking in freedom comes with the responsibility to stay in conversation with God throughout the day, listening for his voice instead of leaning on a list of rules or on our own understanding. So, when the Nazi knocks on your door, what does the Spirit of Christ within tell you to say or do? There is no formula because the answer to your question is based on an intimate relationship with a living Lord who calls you to a disciplined obedience that protects you at all times (and that doesn't mean he protects you from being taken away by the evil at the door).

Perhaps he will tell you not to open the door? Perhaps he will tell you to open the door and speak the exact truth, but he will confuse the evil at the door into hearing something else? The issue is, will you trust Jesus or will you reject his guidance and fall back on your ability to manipulate the circumstances.

### The Cost of Discipleship—

Since my desire is to intimately know Jesus, who the Truth of God in the flesh, I can no longer hide behind lies, masks, innuendo, rationalizations, hypocrisy, denial, or fantasies. I can no longer use defensiveness to distract others from the truth. I will keep my life in the light, regardless of how it may effect my circumstances or reputation (Psalm 119:91).

### Fallen Thinking—

- This compromise won't hurt anyone—in fact, it will help us all get along.
- In comparison, I am much better than she is.
- I don't associate with people who are sinners because I am better than that.
- If I don't lie, he will be hurt.

### Kingdom thinking –

- I have grace for God's reality, not for my fantasies.
- I will live in truth and I will speak truth at all times.
- I embrace the truth because I know it will set me free.
- I live an open and transparent life so that my trust in Jesus can continually be sharpened.
- I will trust God when circumstances seem difficult, not in my manipulation of the circumstances.

### Your Choice?

Will you follow the truth or will you follow a lie? Will you try to hide lies or will you let Jesus expose them? God's grace is poured into reality, not your fantasies? Will you live in the reality of Christ or in the fantasy that you can control your life and circumstances?

# 12

## Becoming Like Jesus through Redemption

*"At this point it becomes evident that when a Christian meets with
injustice, he no longer clings to his rights and defends them at all costs."*

DIETRICH BONHOEFFER

*You have heard that it was said, 'An eye for an eye, and a tooth for a tooth.'
But now I tell you: do not take revenge on someone who wrongs you. If anyone
slaps you on the right cheek, let him slap your left cheek too.*

    *And if someone takes you to court to sue you for your shirt, let him have
your coat as well. And if one of the occupation troops forces you to carry his
pack one mile, carry it two miles. When someone asks you for something, give
it to him; when someone wants to borrow something, lend it to him.*

MATTHEW 5:38-42

Jesus' Objective—*To teach us that our obedient trust in
Jesus can be measured by our demand to get even.*

If you want to follow Jesus, then you must give up your right to take revenge.
Jesus places before you the choice of trusting God to handle the situation or
trusting your own abilities. The choice you make reveals where you place your faith.

    Bonhoeffer notes that the Old Testament established a system of retribu-
tion—"an eye for an eye"—but Jesus, again, pushes his disciples to the *greater
righteousness* required in the kingdom of heaven (Matthew 5:20).

    Think of it like this: You can live in this world and live according to the law,
or you can enter into the kingdom of heaven, subjecting yourself to the standards of grace. If you live according to the law, you will fail. In truth, you already

have. If you follow Jesus into the kingdom of heaven, he will handle the details of the law for you and he will also energize you to live by the higher standard he demands.

Jesus is not repudiating the Old Testament law of retribution, Bonhoeffer writes. He came to fulfill the law, not abolish it. (Matthew 5:17) What Jesus is doing is pushing his disciples into the redemptive realm of grace, where we trust God to defend us and we trust God to redeem us.

And we trust that God knows what to do with our enemies, *even if that means he redeems them, too.*

Would you rather God condemn your enemies or redeem them? Consider the work Jesus must do in us to get us from one side of that question to the other.

## RETRIBUTION IS ROOTED IN REDEMPTION

In truth, the laws on retribution reveal God's redemptive nature because they were established as much to protect the guilty as the innocent. If you take an eye, then those seeking revenge are only allowed to take your eye and nothing more. They cannot completely blind you. They cannot murder you. They are limited in their retribution.

By limiting retribution, the law attempted to bring an end to the cycle of evil that might otherwise escalate: You blind someone in one eye; his kin blind you in both eyes; your kin kill someone from the other clan; and the violent rampage continues (Hebrews 12:15).

Jesus affirms the law, but then, like an arrow pointing toward heaven, he shows how the law is deeply rooted in holiness—God's holiness, not man's meager attempts at holiness. In a sense, Jesus says, "You've heard it said 'an eye for an eye,' but let me clarify the law's intent. God is working to bring an end to the cycle of evil that began with Adam. When Adam's son, Abel, was murdered, his blood cried out for vengeance. When God's son is murdered, his blood will be a proclamation of grace" (paraphrase of Hebrews 12:24 with language suggested from The Message).

"Since God is at work, you do not need to take revenge," Jesus might say. "Our Father will take care of any retribution that is necessary, so I want you to set aside your right to revenge and learn to live according to grace. Follow me into the kingdom life and join me as I invite others to do the same."

## STOP FIGHTING LIKE ORPHANS

Since God is working on retribution, we can stop fighting like creatures that have been abandoned by their Creator, as if our only choice is to deploy weapons of revenge, such as manipulation, blame, shame, hatred, bitterness, pride, gossip, slander, ridicule, threats, deception, violence in anger, and violence with cold-blooded calculation.

These are satanic weapons we use to get our own way without the help of God (2 Corinthians 10:4–5). They just keep us in a cycle of evil-for-evil. Jesus came to end that cycle.

Bonhoeffer says disciples should resist evil in the same way Jesus did on his way to the cross. "Suffering willingly endured is stronger than evil, it spells death to evil," he writes. "The worse the evil, the readier must the Christian be to suffer; he must let the evil person fall into Jesus' hands."

Bonhoeffer also notes that Jesus is not naive about evil, He knows evil firsthand and he is not referring to some esoteric evil in the abstract. He is pushing us to confront evil with faith, looking past the evil doer and the evil act to see God still in control and sitting on his great white throne.

When we suffer evil while maintaining a humble spirit like Christ, we hand our enemies over to Jesus; that is, they are no longer resisting us; instead, they are resisting Jesus. Bonhoeffer says our non-resistance to evil pushes our enemies directly into a confrontation with Jesus.

Bonhoeffer says that any thoughts that Jesus doesn't understand how difficult it is to live in a sinful and fallen world are absurd. *Jesus, you just don't understand how hurtful and aggressive others can be. You don't understand the need to protect yourself!*

Really? Doesn't it show the depth of our delusional thinking that we would say this to a man who, half dead, carried a Roman cross through the streets of Jerusalem, only to have nails driven into his hands and feet before he was hoisted into the air to hang from the cross?

And why? Because he challenged the religious leaders of his day! *Not the political leaders.* And not because he was a revolutionary trying to topple the government. And not because he'd murdered someone, like Barabbas, or stolen from someone, like the thief crucified next to him.

He wasn't crucified for preaching cheap grace: *Let's all just get along. Can't we just try to love each other.* They killed him because his radical message challenged the basic foundation of a system that kept them in charge instead of God.

Jesus placed vengeance back into the hands of the Father, but that doesn't mean he promoted an anemic, victim-like approach to situations where we are wronged. Jesus calls us to respond to evil with belief in his promises; that is, we look past evil into the loving eyes of the Father, where we can see he is at work responding to the ways we've been wronged.

Jesus endured the cross because he saw past the pain into the kingdom of heaven where the Father was waiting for his return. He knew the Father was protecting him within the realm of costly grace, where all things work together for the good of those who are submerged in the love of the Father and submitted to his eternal agenda.

Again, Jesus pushes us to a choice. Are we without a divine defense? Or, is God, the Father looking out for us. When Jeremiah quotes the Father saying, "I know the plans for you and they are not evil," do we believe what God says (Jeremiah 29:11)? God tells us that, in our fallen thinking, we may perceive his plans as evil, but he is working for our God.

Trust God to handle our vengeance? If this seems impractical, Bonhoeffer notes, "Surely we do not wish to accuse Jesus of ignoring the reality and power of evil! Why, the whole of his life was one long conflict with the devil. He calls evil evil, and that is the very reason why he speaks to his followers in this way."

He adds, "We are concerned not with evil in the abstract, but with the *evil person.* Jesus bluntly calls the evil person evil. If I am assailed, I am not to condone or justify aggression. Patient endurance of evil does not mean recognition of its rights."

In other words, to echo the civil rights activist, Martin Luther King Jr., we need to understand the difference between non-violent resistance and non-resistance to evil. We submit, not to abuse, but to God, who draws us into a Spirit-directed response.

"By his willingly renouncing self-defence, the Christian affirms his absolute adherence to Jesus, and his freedom from the tyranny of his own ego," says Bonhoeffer. "The exclusiveness of this adherence is the only power which can overcome evil." In this sense, evil is overcome by our non-violent resistance because it washes over us and crashes into the solid wall of Jesus Christ.

It should be noted that Bonhoeffer wrote *The Cost of Discipleship* while he was being pressured and persecuted by Hitler's Nazi regime. He saw a very real evil emerging, not only in people, but also in the established government of Germany. Bonhoeffer was a pacifist, but he struggled with how a believer should respond when the state had become an instrument of evil.

Bonhoeffer became part of the German Resistance and was peripherally involved in plots to assassinate Hitler. This does nothing to invalidate Bonhoeffer's lessons on revenge, nor does it mean these lessons can only be employed if we adhere to pacifism. The situation in Nazi Germany dealt with the issue of how believers should respond when the government is part of the evil. That question does nothing to release us from placing our faith in God when it comes to personal injustice.

## REDEMPTION, NOT RETRIBUTION

When Jesus hung on the cross, he showed us how to handle revenge. He would not allow anyone or any circumstance to divert him from his objective to lead each and every one of us into the kingdom of heaven and into the presence of God. He remained committed to doing only what the Father told him to do, obediently trusting that God would handle any need for vengeance. If Jesus had stopped to seek revenge against those who had wronged him, he would have been distracted from his holy mission. The truth is, he would have undermined the very thing that the Father sent him to do.

Jesus is on a mission of redemption, not retribution.

God has the better perspective. He knows why things happened and what was intended. He knows who's wronged you. He says there will be a "Vengeance Day," but keep in mind God also knows who you have wronged and who is seeking vengeance against you (Luke 21). He knows who needs to be punished on that day for hurting you, and he also knows what punishment you should receive on that day for the way you have hurt others.

When we take the path of Jonah, insisting that God rain fire down upon our enemies, we are rebelling against the sovereignty of God, who has the right to decide who should be blessed and who should be banished. When we demand an eye for an eye, Jesus holds out his hand, yet does not demand a nail for a nail.

The blood of Jesus "speaks of forgiveness instead of crying out for vengeance like the blood of Abel" (Hebrews 12:24 NLT). When you think of Jesus, do you think of him as taking revenge upon those who hurt him?

The cross shows us how Jesus handled revenge. When you think of Jesus, do you think of him as taking revenge upon those who hurt him?

## GOD AS OUR CHAMPION

God says he won't overlook even the smallest detail; he will hold everyone accountable for what they do: "I will take revenge, I will repay" (Hebrews 10:30; also see Deut 32:35). This freed Jesus from any responsibility related to revenge and it frees you from that responsibility, also. You are now free to do exactly what God tells you to do.

By following Jesus into the kingdom of heaven, we give up our right to revenge. This doesn't mean we're letting any one get away with anything; it simply means we're acknowledging God is sovereign and he has the right to decide when and where and who and how vengeance is taken.

"If we took the precept of non-resistance as an ethical blueprint for general application," Bonhoeffer says, "we should indeed be indulging in idealistic dreams: we should be dreaming of a utopia with laws which the world would never obey. To make non-resistance a principle for secular life is to deny God, by undermining his gracious ordinance for the preservation of the world."

But Bonhoeffer adds that Jesus isn't setting up a blueprint for civil authority; rather, "he is the one who vanquished evil through suffering. It looked as though evil had triumphed on the cross, but the real victory belonged to Jesus." Without the cross, what Jesus teaches would be wholly impractical; with the cross, it is the only significant response to evil because the cross is what gives power to our non-resistance to evil. "And only such obedience is blessed with the promise that we shall be partakers of Christ's victory as well as of his sufferings," says Bonhoeffer.

## GETTING EVEN IS A FAITHLESS ACT

When we take vengeance into our own hands, we slander the heart of God and reveal our lack of faith. But far worse, we condemn ourselves to a shallow faith because we will never be able to see how God sweeps in to protect us. The trust is that Jesus is our champion—our mediator and advocate before God. The trust is that the unseen God sees our predicament and the obedience is believing that he is doing something about it.

This changes the way we live because we become more certain that God will do what he says he will do. It will drive us into a deeper faith, deeper into the "more faithful" obedience required to enter the kingdom of heaven.

Will you give your revenge to God and believe his response to those who have hurt you will be greater than any "eye for an eye" response of your own? The idea is that you give God your rights and trust that he will take care of your needs. In faith, we believe that vengeance is mine, says the Lord.

Will God take care of it? Here is the faith element. It takes an incredible amount of faith to believe God will do that. We want to be angry; we want to hit back; we want to teach those who hurt us a lesson; we want justice.

## JESUS GAVE UP HIS RIGHTS

Jesus gave up his rights. If you want to be like Jesus, then you must give up your rights, too, trusting that God is looking out for you just as he looked out for Jesus (Philippians 2:7).

When you follow Jesus, you must give up your right to take revenge, to be treated with respect, your right to security and safety, to control the details of your life; your right to hold back anything when someone comes to you in need. This means you give up the right to be treated fairly, to be understood, the right to be considered important, to be in control, the right to be disengaged, to be self-absorbed, and the right to serve others only at your own convenience.

It also means you give up the right to remain independent from Jesus and other believers—the body of Christ. You give up the right to your sins, those nasty and those merely naughty. Most of all, you give up your right to be in rebellion to God because you cannot serve God while trying to be God. You cannot cling to your rights while claiming to give everything to Christ.

The argument rising in you right now that says this isn't fair or even feasible is a test of your faith: if you give your rights to God, he will be your champion? Discipleship isn't about what is fair or feasible. Fairness is based on perspective; feasibility is based on what we can figure out.

We make the same arguments with God. We plead for fairness when we're really asking for special treatment. But God can say to us: "I'm a Holy God and you've done some very unholy things. Fair means I can stay angry at you forever and punish you for the horrible things you've done. Fair means I can give you every bit of what you deserve. Do you really want fair?"

While we're pleading fairness, God, knowing what *fair* would lead to, pursues us with an unfailing, unfair love: "He has not punished us for all our sins, nor does he deal with us as we deserve" (Psalm 103:10 NLT).

## NO MORE TIT-FOR-TAT

Jesus says that in the kingdom of heaven, rather than submitting to the law, you now submit to the law of grace. Jesus says that in the kingdom of heaven your focus is no longer on yourself but on others. When someone tries to humiliate you, Jesus says confront him with your humility (Matthew 5:39). When someone tries to take what is yours, Jesus says confront her by giving even more. Instead of demanding security, Jesus says we should voluntarily give away the things we normally hold back to protect us in the future (Matthew 5:40). Instead of demanding freedom, Jesus says we should voluntarily carry the burdens of others. "And if one of the occupation troops forces you to carry his pack one mile, carry it two miles" (Matthew 5:41).

Bonhoeffer says, "Violence stands condemned by its failure to evoke counter-violence. When a man unjustly demands that I should give him my coat, I offer him my cloak also, and so counter his demand; when he requires me to go the other mile, I go willingly, and show up his exploitation of my service for what it is."

In a sense, Jesus is saying, "I have better things for you to do than to chase after revenge. I want you focused on kingdom work, helping me to bring others into the kingdom. So don't be foolish! Revenge is a job that our Father set aside for himself. Do you really think you can do a better job than God at getting even? Do you really want to get in the way of God when he is handling revenge for you?"

It's the kind of faith David showed when he approached Goliath, saying, "You come against me with sword and spear and javelin, but I come against you in the name of the Lord Almighty, the God of the armies of Israel, whom you have defied" (1 Samuel 17:45 NIV).

It's the kind of obedient trust in Jesus you will be challenged to show the next time someone wrongs you or unjustly demands something from you.

❧

### The Cost of Discipleship—

Jesus calls you to respond to evil with an obedient trust in his promises. You must give up your right to take revenge and trust God for retribution or redemption.

### Fallen Thinking—

- This person deserves to be paid back for the evil he's done to me!
- No one else is looking out for me, so I have to do it myself.
- If I don't seek revenge, she will get away with it.
- I am only doing what is fair.

### Kingdom Thinking—

- Jesus has better things for me to do than to chase after revenge.
- I have been wronged, but I will trust God to make it right.
- I have made my share of mistakes and offenses, so I wouldn't want to give to someone what I deserve.
- God knows what to do with my enemies, even if that means he redeems them, too.

### Your Choice?

Why would you want to take retribution into you own hands instead of trusting the God of the universe to handle it? Will you trust that vengeance belongs to God or will you insist on getting even? (Romans 12:19)

# 13

## BECOMING LIKE JESUS
## WHEN FACING ENEMIES

*"Love is defined in uncompromising terms as the love of our enemies. Had*
*Jesus only told us to love our brethren, we might have misunderstood what he*
*meant by love, but now he leaves us in no doubt whatever as to his meaning."*
DIETRICH BONHOEFFER

*You have heard that it was said, 'Love your friends, hate your enemies.' But*
*now I tell you: love your enemies and pray for those who persecute you, so that*
*you may become the children of your Father in heaven. For he makes his sun*
*to shine on bad and good people alike, and gives rain to those who do good*
*and to those who do evil. Why should God reward you if you love only the*
*people who love you? Even the tax collectors do that! And if you speak only to*
*your friends, have you done anything out of the ordinary? Even the pagans do*
*that! You must be perfect—just as your Father in heaven is perfect.*
MATTHEW 5:43-48

Jesus' Objective—*To teach us that our trust in Jesus can*
*be measured by the way we love our enemies.*

The Sermon on the Mount can be summed up in one word: love.
Jesus said we should love God, love our neighbor, love ourselves—and
also love our enemies. The idea of loving our enemies wasn't a radical new
command from Jesus. It was part of the Levitical code ("Do not take revenge on
others or continue to hate them, but love your neighbors as you love yourself.
I am the Lord"—Leviticus 19:18), and also a feature of Old Testament wisdom
("If your enemies are hungry, feed them; if they are thirsty, give them a drink.

You will make them burn with shame, and the Lord will reward you"—Proverbs 25:21-22).

The religious leaders were teaching their disciples to love friends, but hate enemies and so Jesus, again, confronts their hypocrisy. Like the hiss of the snake, the religious leaders were changing the law to suit themselves because the Old Testament never says, "hate your enemies." Jesus is unmerciful in contrasting the truth of God against the false religion of the Pharisees.

And Jesus is absolutely relentless in pushing the standards of the law to a higher level; in truth, the level at which they've always been in the kingdom of heaven. In this case, he speaks about the law of love, insisting it must be a love that is extraordinary and remarkable.

Bonhoeffer notes he calls us to a sacrificial love where we love our enemies in exactly the same way we love our friends. Yet, he adds, "By our enemies Jesus means those who are quite intractable and utterly unresponsive to our love, who forgive us nothing when we forgive them all, who requite our love with hatred and our service with derision."

Our enemies may reject our love; they may waste our love, discount our love, and react angrily to our love. They may never understand our love or even be changed through our love; yet, Jesus calls us to love them without these guarantees. In doing this, he is calling us to become more like him: "While we were still sinners, Christ died for us" (Romans 5:8 NIV).

This is the kind of love that asks nothing in return, notes Bonhoeffer; yet, seeks those who need it. "And who needs our love more than those who are consumed with hatred and are utterly devoid of love?," he asks. "Who in other words deserves our love more than our enemy? Where is love more glorified than where she dwells in the midst of her enemies?"

Steve Pettit, director of One in Christ Ministries, commonly refers to God's love as a love that needs no "because." God doesn't give his love because of something we've done; he doesn't give his love because of something he might gain; and he doesn't give his love because we deserve it. He just gives his love—because. God's very nature is love ("God is love"—1 John 4:16).

It is a love beyond human understanding. "We can understand someone dying for a person worth dying for, and we can understand how someone good and noble could inspire us to selfless sacrifice," says the apostle Paul. "But God put his love on the line for us by offering his Son in sacrificial death while we were of no use to him" (Romans 5:7-8 MSG).

We are only able to love our enemies because God's love flows through us. And this is what makes our love extraordinary, a love that shows we are living in the kingdom of heaven and trusting that even the worst of our enemies is not beyond the power of God's power to change lives.

John MacArthur says this extraordinary love is only possible when Jesus injects costly grace into a believer's life: "It is the spirit Abraham manifested when he gave the best land to his nephew Lot. It is the spirit of Joseph when he embraced and kissed the brothers who had so terribly wronged him. It is the spirit that would not let David take advantage of the opportunity to take the life of Saul, who was then seeking to take David's life. It is the spirit that led Elisha to feed the enemy Assyrian army. It is the spirit that led Stephen to pray for those who were stoning him to death".[9]

Bonhoeffer says Christ calls us to love our enemies with the same love we would have for a precious lover. "The Christian must treat his enemy as a brother, and requite his hostility with love," says Bonhoeffer. "His behaviour must be determined not by the way others treat him, but by the treatment he himself receives from Jesus; it has only one source, and that is the will of Jesus."

Jesus enables us to love our enemies with patience, kindness, encouragement, humility, service, trust, truth, hope, perseverance, and joy (1 Corinthians 13:1-13). Costly grace creates in us a love that is sincere, service-oriented and Spirit-directed. It allows us to approach those who oppose us faithful in prayer, generous in invitation, and full of blessings for them (Romans 12:9-21).

This kind of love "cuts right across [our] ideas of good and evil," says Bonhoeffer. It is offensive to us to think in this way, but it is a sure sign we are entering the kingdom of heaven when we begin to see our enemies with the eyes of Jesus, understanding that God's way to defeat them is by loving them.

Fallen men and women cannot do this, only those who carry Jesus within and who respond obediently to the commands of Jesus. Only those who obediently believe in Jesus can love with the love of God flowing through them. Otherwise, their love is a diminished love that lacks the power to overcome evil, a shadow love that mixes selfish motives—perhaps in the face of an enemy the motive of self-preservation—with unqualified, godly motives.

Bonhoeffer says Jesus calls us to a love that makes no distinction between one enemy or the other and no distinction between a private enemy or a public one (that is, someone we personally know or someone, say, in public office whose policies are designed to harm us). Regardless we are to offer unqualified love to our enemies. We're to bless them, do good for them and pray for them.

## LOVE YOUR ENEMIES

Jesus commands us to an active love of our enemies. Our love is more than just a passive bearing of persecution and hatred. We must engage in loving our enemies by blessing them, doing good for them, and praying for them regardless of who they are or what they have done. Bonhoeffer says, "We are not to imagine that this is to condone his evil; such a love proceeds from strength rather than weakness, from truth rather than fear, and therefore it cannot be guilty of the hatred of another."

It is a fearless love, where we recognize God loved us even when we were his enemies, and now, by his love within us, we can love our enemies with the same love aimed at redemption.

But do you see how this is related to our faith, when we know, and obediently trust, that God is determined to love the sin and fallenness out of us, we can then act upon our faith by determining to love the sin and fallenness out of our enemies. We start allowing the love of Christ to flow through us, driving away the cycle of fear that keeps us locked in hostility with our enemies. In this way, we are conformed to the image of Christ instead of the image of our enemies (Romans 12:2).

## DO GOOD TO THOSE WHO HATE YOU

We are to love in deed as well as word. Jesus calls us to an active love. The apostle Paul says, "If your enemies are hungry, feed them; if they are thirsty, give them a drink; for by doing this you will make them burn with shame" (Romans 12:20).

Doing this is humanly impossible, but it brings you daily to the door of dependence upon Jesus, where you must draw upon his strength to love those who hate you: "To this end I labor, struggling with all his energy, which so powerfully works in me" (Colossians 1:29 NIV).

It requires faith to do the good works Jesus requires of us as we face our enemies, where we enter their lives by showing them the uncommon compassion of Jesus.

## PRAY FOR THOSE WHO PERSECUTE YOU

Bonhoeffer says, "If our enemy cannot put up with us any longer and takes to cursing us, our immediate reaction must be to lift up our hands and bless him." Bonhoeffer notes that, through prayer, we can stand by our enemy's side and plead for him to God. This doesn't mean they won't hurt us or persecute us, but it shows they cannot overcome us. Like Jesus, we take "their distress and poverty, their guilt and perdition upon ourselves," says Bonheoffer.

When they insult us, it only draws us closer to God and them closer to reconciliation. But this requires us to obediently trust that Jesus is working through us and requires that we abandon ourselves to his will, allowing him to make us an instrument of reconciliation even if it causes us pain or hardship

The cross is a reminder that we were once Christ's enemies. How did he treat us? We were overcome by the love of Jesus and now with his love flowing through us, our eyes can be opened to seeing our enemies as brothers and sisters as equally in need of redemption as we are.

How then does love conquer?

Our enemy takes us "along the way of the cross and into fellowship with the Crucified" (Bonhoeffer). The more we are persecuted, the more certain the victory of Jesus because his love will take over where ours fails.

We were the enemies of Jesus and he overcame us by his love. We must see our enemies in the same way. Our enemies are the object of God's love in the same way we were. We cannot be disciples of Jesus and continue to live and love at the world's level. We are called to an extraordinary life and that includes expressing an extraordinary love.

The deeper we forge into what Bonhoeffer calls "the holy struggle," the more we realize how crucial it is for us to love our enemies and give up on exacting our own revenge. The person who wants to follow Christ in discipleship must cling to the Lord and prepare for that battle. "The time is coming when the confession of the living God will incur not only the hatred and the fury of the world . . . but complete ostracism from 'human society,'" Bonhoeffer notes. Anyone who pays attention to the news cannot help but realize we are in an age of spreading and intensifying persecution of those who value Christ above all else.

We pray for our enemies by crying out to God for their peace. We remember that we once were confused and shipwrecked by sin, and we should earnestly desire our enemies find the same deliverance and freedom Christ has given us. What could we do ourselves that would pierce the heart of an enemy more severely than pray down the redemption of Christ on their souls?

⋘⋙

## The Cost of Discipleship—
You can no longer love according to the world's definition of love. You must let God define your love and you must give love to anyone and everyone unconditionally.

## Fallen Thinking—
- My enemies need to be sneered out of their fears.
- I will love others when they deserve it, appreciate it, respond well to it, etc.
- Yes, I trust Jesus but surely he doesn't mean for me to love my (ex-wife, obnoxious neighbor, lying co-worker, etc.)
- He does not deserve my love; she is beyond even God's love.

## Kingdom Thinking—
- My enemies need to be loved out of their fears.
- I will love others because they need it.
- I was once an enemy of God. God can redeem my enemies the same way he has redeemed me.
- I will love my enemies because I believe Jesus more than I believe my fears.

## Your Choice?
Will you obediently trust Jesus and love your enemy in the same way you love your brother or sister? Or will you love selectively and according to your own definition of love?

# 14

## Becoming Like Jesus in Quiet Service

*"All that the follower of Jesus has to do is to make sure that his obedience, following and love are entirely spontaneous and unpremeditated.... Otherwise you are simply displaying your own virtue, and not that which has its source in Jesus Christ."*

Dietrich Bonhoeffer

*Make certain you do not perform your religious duties in public so that people will see what you do. If you do these things publicly, you will not have any reward from your Father in heaven. So when you give something to a needy person, do not make a big show of it, as the hypocrites do in the houses of worship and on the streets. They do it so that people will praise them. I assure you, they have already been paid in full. But when you help a needy person, do it in such a way that even your closest friend will not know about it. Then it will be a private matter. And your Father, who sees what you do in private, will reward you.*

Matthew 6:1-4

Jesus' Objective—*To teach us that our service flows from Jesus through us to others, so when our motives are self-centered, we block the other-centered love of Christ from flowing through us. To teach us that the kingdom of heaven is not limited to the things we see.*

The cost of discipleship is that we must put an end to our spiritual pride. We must ruthlessly abandon any attempts to be good or appear good on our own. Our good deeds must flow from our connection to Jesus and not the other

way around. We bring no goodness to him and we must reject any thoughts that
suggest otherwise.

Bonhoeffer says that so far in his sermon Jesus has taught that being his discipleship means:

**We are separated from the world**—We are separated from the world but not
like cloistered monks withdrawn from the world; rather, as a people set apart by
God to become like his Son. (Romans 8:29-30) We are in the world, but not of
the world, separated from others by the Holy Spirit working within us, yet interacting with others because we are in union with Christ, the mediator between
God and fallen man.

**We transcend human standards**—The work of Jesus in us transcends our
own standards of righteousness and, although he gives his righteousness to us,
following him will often lead us to do more than the law requires. We must go
the extra mile.

**We live extraordinary lives**—We are extraordinary because of Christ working
through us. We can no longer live average lives because we are now in union with
Jesus; we live with a constant, real connection to God's divine nature.

And because there is a danger we will become impressed with our own piety
and service to God, Jesus says we must be visible in our Christian character but
invisible in Christian service. "Be especially careful when you are trying to be good
so that you don't make a performance out of it," says Jesus. "It might be good
theater, but the God who made you won't be applauding" (Matthew 6:1 MSG).

Jesus continues to get us ready for the kingdom of heaven. In a sense, he says
once we pass through the narrow gate, we won't think about how it looks—good
or bad—when we stop to help others. We'll just do it, allowing the love of Jesus
to spontaneously pour out of us into the lives of others.

The problem is, when we start thinking about how our service looks or who it
might impress, we've changed the nature of what we're doing. It's no longer an
act of love and that means it's no longer noticeable in the kingdom of heaven.

Bonhoeffer notes there is an obvious temptation to "mistake Christ's work for
a commendation of a new, however novel, free and inspiring pattern for pious
living. How eagerly would the religious embrace a life of poverty, truthfulness

and suffering, if only they might thereby satisfy their yearning not only to be-lieve, but to see with their own eyes!"

## WE ARE CALLED TO LOVE THE WORLD UP-CLOSE

But Jesus doesn't call us to be good, little Christians. And we do not become Christian or holy through our piety, regardless of how pure our motives when we pursue holiness. The things we do, the prayers we pray, the service we offer to others do not make us holy and when we think and act like they do, we are embracing heresy, plain and simple.

At the same time, Bonhoeffer notes, Jesus says nothing about abandoning the world, separating ourselves from others in a monistic fashion, such as creating our Christian ghettos and Jesus sub-cultures.

Jesus will have nothing to do with an impractical religion that establishes a contrived environment where it is easy to love the world at a distance. He calls us to a blood and sweat faith where we daily encounter what Peter Lord commonly calls the "nasty now-and-now" of life.[10]

Jesus didn't leave the comfort of heaven to get dirty and bloody and hurt just so we could live out a mythological Christianity of the sweet-by-and-by. A Christianity of goodness and good feeling, where people see us and declare us to be nice people. *Aren't they special? Aren't they extraordinary?*

And when we receive such praise, we are stealing from Jesus.

## MENIAL WAS NOT BENEATH JESUS

Where Jesus is taking us is to a place where we are so focused on serving the needs of others that it is impossible for us to remain self-centered. "Do nothing out of selfish ambition . . ." Paul says, "But in humility consider others better than yourselves" (Philippians 2:3 NIV).

Jesus set the example when "of his own free will he gave up all he had, and took the nature of a servant"; when he got up from the meal and then got down on his knees to wash his disciples' feet (Philippians 2:7a; John 13:4–5). He placed the needs of others above his own, even as he approached his darkest hour. "Now that I, your Lord and Teacher, have washed your feet, you also should wash one another's feet" (John 13:14 NIV).

And so Jesus calls us to always be vigilant in examining the motives of our Christian service. Our "better righteousness" should never be about bringing praise to ourselves and the best way to prevent that is to never focus on what people will think when we do something for others, yet to always do what Jesus tells us to do.

Jesus insists we surrender our motives to his righteousness, where our old self is crucified and the ego is no longer central. That way, what emerges from the inside of us is the righteousness of Jesus, not our own mere good intentions.

## GENUINE LOVE IS ALWAYS SELF-FORGETFUL

"Genuine love is always self-forgetful in the true sense of the word," says Bonhoeffer. "But if we are to have it, our old man must die with all his virtues and qualities, and this can only be done where the disciple forgets self and clings solely to Christ. . . . The love of Christ crucified, who delivers our old man to death, is the love which lives in those who follow him."

The apostle Paul explains: *"It is no longer I who live, but it is Christ who lives in me. This life that I live now, I live by faith in the Son of God, who loved me and gave his life for me"* (Galatians 2:20).

Our service to others should be an act of worship (Romans 12:1-3) and when we draw attention to ourselves, we're no longer worshiping God; we're actually creating a situation where others will worship us. Is there any doubt why this would be offensive to God?

In addition, you might start comparing the way one act of service compares to another. *Who wants to give chocolate bars to the kids vs. who wants to clean the bed pans?*

It also means you might start doing things that bring you more praise and it might mean you will start doing only the things you like to do. You might want to help some and not others. *Why does that Jesus hang out with sinners? It looks so bad? It is a waste of his talents?*

Bonhoeffer says the extraordinary life that comes from being a disciple is a natural fruit of obedience. When we stay focused on Jesus, we will find we are living extraordinary lives. But when we begin to focus on the "extraordinary quality of the Christian life," then we're no longer following Christ."

We submit to the sovereignty of Jesus and our obedience leads us to a life extraordinary as our hearts begin to beat as one with his. When we obey Jesus, we line up with his thoughts and his plans. Our agenda, our focus, and our desires become one with his and, as a result, the things we do for others in the name of Jesus become second nature to us. We do them without thinking about what others may think or how we may be rewarded.

### The Cost of Discipleship—

My service flows from God through Jesus through me to others. I must serve others from the life of Jesus flowing through me even if it is inconvenient or unpleasant, even if no one will ever know, even if those I serve never say thank you.

### Fallen Thinking—

- I must impress God and others with my ability to serve others.
- I will only serve others after I have met my own needs and if it is convenient to my schedule or plans.
- I must be told 'well done' by others in public.
- God must constantly tell me he is looking out for me, or I will doubt he really cares about what I am doing.

### Kingdom Thinking—

- I seek Jesus first and let my service flow from my intimate trust in him.
- I do not do for God, rather God does through me.
- I serve wherever the life of Christ directs me to serve and I will faithful wait for my 'well done' to come from God in that secret place.
- I do not have to see God to know that he cares about me and is actively involved in my life.
- I don't have to receive an immediate blessing from God because I know he will reward me beyond my imagination in heaven.

## Your Choice?

Jesus has placed his life inside you and his objective is to love others through you even as you keep learning how much he loves you. Your choice is based upon obedience; if you trust Jesus, then you will find it easy to be obedient to his commands and the promptings he gives you each day.

Will you obediently trust Jesus and let his life flow through you to serve others? Or will you try to serve others in your own strength? The answer seems obvious, but the obedience of intimacy is to see your choice this way when you're in the middle of the "*nasty now-and-now*" of life.

# 15

## BECOMING LIKE JESUS IN PRAYER

*"True prayer does not depend either on the individual or the whole
body of the faithful, but solely upon the knowledge that our heavenly
Father knows our needs. That makes God the sole object of our prayers,
and frees us from a false confidence in our own prayerful efforts."*

DIETRICH BONHOEFFER

*When you pray, do not be like the hypocrites! They love to stand up and pray
in the houses of worship and on the street corners, so that everyone will see
them. I assure you, they have already been paid in full. But when you pray,
go to your room, close the door, and pray to your Father, who is unseen. And
your Father, who sees what you do in private, will reward you.*

*When you pray, do not use a lot of meaningless words, as the pagans
do, who think that their gods will hear them because their prayers are long.
Do not be like them. Your Father already knows what you need before you
ask him.*

MATTHEW 6:5-8

*Jesus' Objective—To teach us that prayer is an intimate conversation,
where we come to know the loving nature of our heavenly Father and develop
an intimate trust in him. Trying to impress others with our prayers or using
prayer merely to get things from God is a sign we have lost our focus.*

Prayer is an intimate conversation with your heavenly Father. When you try
to impress others with your ability to pray, you mock that intimacy.
You appear to be focusing on the Father when you're actually focusing on
yourself—*your* needs, *your* wants, *your* ability to persuade and bully God, and

*your* desire to impress others with your knowledge of how to get God to give you what you want when you want it.

It's absolutely no different from standing up and saying, "Look at me so you can be impressed with how connected I am with God!"

Eugene Peterson paraphrases Jesus' comments this way, "The world is full of so-called prayer warriors who are prayer-ignorant. They're full of formulas and programs and advice, peddling techniques for getting what you want from God. Don't fall for that nonsense. This is your Father you are dealing with, and he knows better than you what you need" (Matthew 6:7-8 MSG).

If your motivation in prayer is to impress people, then Jesus says you will get what you want: praise from other people. In truth, that is exactly what you are asking for when you pray to impress: 'Give me the praise of others.' Since your behavior exposes your beliefs, the presumption with prayers like this must be that praise from people can be used to pay bills or get you out of a jam when you're flat on your back in the middle of some mess.

Jesus indicates God sees no need to reward you for these self-promoting prayers. They represent worldly thinking. Why would God reward you for that when he wants you to pray like someone who is part of the kingdom of heaven?

In truth, God wants you to talk to him as if you are a member of his family because, as a disciple of Jesus, you are part of God's family. Bonheoffer notes a disciple's prayers should be like a child talking with his father. A child doesn't have to impress his father (or anyone else) to get him to listen and respond to his requests.

A child doesn't have to jump through hoops (like do good works) to convince the father to take care of his needs. If we, as bad as we are, know how to give good things to our children, how much more, then, will our Father in heaven "give good things to those who ask him" (based on Matthew 7:11).

"The right way to approach God is to stretch out our hands and ask of One who we know has the heart of a Father," says Bonhoeffer. Jesus says the Father knows our needs even before we ask and that is an important element to remember when we approach God in prayer. If someone already knows our needs, then, when we talk to him, we can just talk; there is no need to think through a presentation.

"If God were ignorant of our needs, we should have to think out beforehand *how* we should tell him about them, *what we* should tell him, and whether we should tell him or not. Thus faith, which is the mainspring of Christian prayer, excludes all reflection and premeditation," says Bonhoeffer. In other words, the prayer of a disciple can be spontaneous and confident, knowing we can approach the throne of grace confidently. Bonhoeffer notes that Jesus is proof that God wants such intimacy with us. He came to create a bridge to God and we become intimate with the Father through Jesus.

This is another problem with prayers of pride. They set us up to be *false mediators* between others and God. They slyly say, "Look at how I pray. Watch me and see how persuasive I can be with God." They suggest we have a special connection with God independent of our connection through Christ, and that encourages others to believe our prayers have more meaning before God than their prayers—when the *gospel* truth is, anyone connected to God through Jesus can approach *the throne of grace* boldly (Hebrews 4:16).

"Christian prayer presupposes faith, that is, adherence to Christ," says Bonhoeffer. "He is the one and only Mediator of our prayers. We pray at his command, and to that word Christian prayer is always bound." This is the reason we pray in the name of Jesus and why eliminating the name of Jesus from our prayers is a significant theological issue.

It is important to note, then, the distinct difference between being an intercessor for others and any arrogant attempt to be a mediator for them. We do not connect anyone to God; Jesus connects them to God. But Jesus calls us to intercede on behalf of others, standing beside and sometimes standing instead as we fulfill the law of Christ by carrying the burdens of others to God in prayer (Galatians 6:2).

Bonhoeffer says, "It matters little what form of prayer we adopt or how many words we use, what matters is the faith which lays hold on God and touches the heart of the Father who knew us long before we came to him."

Prayer is not a tool for getting things from God; no more than a conversation is simply a means for ordering meals at the drive-through window. Our modern approach to prayer is to look at it like just another piece of technology. We place our order with God by speaking into the device of prayer thus reducing the Master and Creator of the universe to a mere order-taker.

Jesus will not allow such a trivial view of prayer. He commands that we keep it intimate, and nearly every prayer he utters in the New Testament begins with

ABBA, an affectionate name for a tender, loving father. This is why he says not to ramble on with repetitive words like the pagans do. We wouldn't do that in a conversation with someone we loved and honored; why would we do that when we speak in intimate conversation with the Father?

Jesus is showing us that relationships in the kingdom of heaven are lovingly other-focused and this is reflected in the way we pray. Bonhoeffer says prayer is the antithesis of self-display. We focus on God and not on ourselves. By focusing on God, who he is and what he can do, our problems become smaller and his power to deal with them becomes larger. Of course, it has always been that way, but we have been thinking like mortal men and not thinking like eternal beings who reside in the kingdom of heaven.

What do your prayers say about the way you view God?

What do your prayers say about your faith in God?

What do you prayers say about your love-obedience to Jesus?

*This, then, is how you should pray: "Our Father in heaven: May your holy name be honored; may your Kingdom come; may your will be done on earth as it is in heaven. Give us today the food we need. Forgive us the wrongs we have done, as we forgive the wrongs that others have done to us. Do not bring us to hard testing, but keep us safe from the Evil One.*

*If you forgive others the wrongs they have done to you, your Father in heaven will also forgive you. But if you do not forgive others, then your Father will not forgive the wrongs you have done"* (Matthew 6:9-15).

Jesus teaches the disciples to pray . . .

### *"Our Father in heaven"*
The call of Jesus binds us into the family of God. We are now brothers and sisters, joint-heirs through Jesus. And Jesus shows this by shifting from *my father* to *our father*. God is our father, too, and we are part of the family of God, a community of Christ-followers.

### *"May your holy name be honored"*
We're to acknowledge God's sovereignty and power before asking for anything. Otherwise, we're likely to maximize our problems and minimize God's greatness and we also minimize—*in our minds*—God's ability to handle our problems.

*"May your kingdom come"*

When we pray, we are praying the kingdom of heaven into our circumstances. We are acknowledging God's sovereignty and his control over the situation. We are adjusting our thinking to the kingdom of heaven. Bonhoeffer says this reminds us each day, "God's name, God's kingdom, God's will must be the primary object of Christian prayer. Of course it is not as if God needed our prayers, but they are the means by which the disciples become partakers in the heavenly treasure for which they pray."

*"Give us today the food we need"*

Even in our prayers, we are brought to a choice. Will we believe that God will provide? Our prayers move us into kingdom thinking, where we acknowledge that God provides everything we have—that is, even our daily bread does not come from the mere work of our hands, from our own talents and abilities. God is our provider, no matter who *hands us* our daily bread.

*"Forgive us the wrongs we have done*

. . . As we forgive the wrongs that others have done to us." Bonhoeffer says, "Living as they do in fellowship with him, [Christ's followers] ought to be sinless, but in practice their life is marred daily with all manner of unbelief, sloth in prayer, lack of bodily discipline, self-indulgence of every kind, envy, hatred and ambition. No wonder that they must pray daily for God's forgiveness."

The command of Jesus, even as it shows up in prayer, is clear and unambiguous: If you forgive those who sin against you, then God will forgive you for your sins against him. If you maintain an unforgiving attitude, then God will not forgive you for your sins. The question is not *should, if, or can someone be forgiven*; the test of your faith is, will you make the choice to forgive?

*"Do not bring us to hard testing*

. . . But keep us safe from the Evil One." We confront the enemy in God's strength; humbly, knowing God is the source of our authority to push back the evil one. This prayer, in a sense, says, "Train me so that when I face conflict, discouragement, or temptation—when I collide with any obstacle—I rely on you and you alone."

Temptation is not a sin, but it becomes sin when I focus on the temptation and not God, who has the power to deliver me from the temptation. He gives us the ability to take our thoughts captive in Christ.

### "For thine is the kingdom"

Bonhoeffer says, by praying like this, "The disciples are renewed in their assurance that the kingdom is God's by their fellowship in Jesus Christ, on whom depends the fulfillment of all their prayers. In him God's name is hallowed, his kingdom comes and his will is done."

"For his sake the disciples are preserved in body and receive forgiveness of sin, in his strength they are preserved in all times of temptation, in his power they are delivered and brought to eternal life," says Bonhoeffer. "His is the kingdom and the power and the glory for ever and ever in the unity of the Father."

Our prayers re-affirm we are God's children. He is our Father and we live within his kingdom and under his protection. We know in the kingdom his will will be done and his promises will be fulfilled. We can rest in that certainty.

We are not only citizens in the kingdom; we are part of God's family—not because we deserve it, but because we are in fellowship with Jesus. We can trust he will see to it that his name is glorified in us. We may be tempted and struggle with sin, yet we know the Father will provide his strength to deliver us. God's name is holy, the Kingdom belongs to him, and in sovereignty his will is going to be done.

We do not need to know how prayer works or why. This only serves to take our focus off Jesus; rather, we need to know that Jesus works within us to give us Christlike character and to bring us through the narrow gate into the kingdom of heaven. Prayer prepares us for the kingdom by teaching us, not only how God thinks, but also by showing us his will in action.

◈

### The Cost of Discipleship—

You must adjust your prayers to seek intimacy with the Father and he will take care of everything else. "Steep your life in God-reality, God-initiative, God-provisions. Don't worry about missing out. You'll find all your everyday human concerns will be met" (Matthew 6:33 MSG). If you believed without a doubt that God heard your prayers and would specifically answer them, how would you pray? Start praying that way.

### Fallen Thinking—

- I'm not sure God will answer my prayers, so I'd better have a back-up plan.
- In fact, it would probably be best to make God the back-up plan and go with my solution first.

### Kingdom Thinking—

- I will seek you and your kingdom first—You will supply all I need. You know what I need and when I need it.

### Your Choice?

Self-centered prayers are a signal you need to mature toward God-centered prayer. The issue is not what you are doing wrong; rather, Jesus is providing a measurement so you can plainly see when you are out of alignment with him. Don't get stuck on your failure; instead, follow Jesus into an intimate prayer life where you focus on God and join him in his love for others.

Will you, in obedient faith, use prayer to enter into an intimate conversation with the Father? Or, will you use prayer as a tool for getting what you want or showing others how clever you are? Next time you pray, think about the intimate conversation.

# 16

## Becoming Like Jesus
## in Spiritual Disciplines

*"When all is said and done, the life of faith is nothing if not an unending
struggle of the spirit with every available weapon against the flesh."*

DIETRICH BONHOEFFER

*And when you fast, do not put on a sad face as the hypocrites do. They neglect
their appearance so that everyone will see that they are fasting. I assure you,
they have already been paid in full. When you go without food, wash your
face and comb your hair, so that others cannot know that you are fasting—
only your Father, who is unseen, will know. And your Father, who sees what
you do in private, will reward you.*

MATTHEW 6:16-18

Jesus' Objective—*To teach us that our spiritual habits should help
us develop intimacy with the Father, not praise for ourselves.*

Have you ever had a question in your mind about how deeply Jesus was
devoted to the Father? Don't we tend to see it as a given that Jesus was
totally devoted to the Father?

The truth is, Jesus had to be totally devoted to the Father for him to be who he
was and to do what he did. In addition, Jesus didn't have to show everyone how
devoted he was to the Father because his relentless obedience to the Father's will
was proof enough. Jesus focused on the Father and trusted with certainty that
the Father would see what he was doing and would reward him for his faithful
obedience.

If you want to be like Jesus, then the thing to do is to follow him into a relent-less obedience to God's will and to stop drawing attention to yourself and your own spirituality. Focus on pleasing the Father and not pleasing yourself or pleas-ing those around you. Don't try to prove your devotion to God, just show God you are devoted to him.

In this passage, Jesus continues to contrast life in this world with life in the king-dom of heaven, and it should come as no surprise, he is moving you toward a choice.

In essence, he says, if you want to live by the standards of this world, then make a big show about your devotion to God. When you fast, act like you are carrying the weight of the world on your shoulders. Give yourself that ruffled look, like you haven't had a meal in days and you're really suffering for it. Tell everyone you're on a special fast, waiting to hear from God or demanding that the Almighty give you a spiritual breakthrough.

If you choose to live this way, you *will* impress people. They *will* see you as godly. You might even impress yourself. But you won't be impressing God be-cause he sees into your heart and he knows the pride and fear you harbor there. The affirmation and adulation that you get from others will be your reward, but that's all you're going to get.

You can't be rewarded in the kingdom of heaven for your devotion because you made a choice to follow the rules of this world and not the rules of the king-dom. That would be like expecting to be rewarded with an Olympic gold medal for fasting when you actually competed in an NCAA tournament. The venue is different; the standards are different; and the judges are different.

We wouldn't even attempt to argue that the winner of an NCAA tournament should be rewarded with an Olympic gold medal, so why do we think God should reward us when we do things according to this world's rules rather than according to the higher standards of the kingdom?

There is another choice. If you want to be rewarded in the kingdom (and if you want to be like Jesus), then go about your fasting quietly. Let the joy of the Lord naturally emerge on your face. Dress like you usually do and then make your way through the day in such a way that no one will look at you and wonder when you had your last meal.

You don't have to tell others you've skipped a meal or two. You don't even have to tell God. He already knows. Perhaps we see the gentle humor of Jesus in his patient explanation that the God who is unseen is perfectly capable of seeing. If he isn't able to see what we're doing, then he really isn't God. The truth is, he sees directly into our hearts and he knows whether we are partially or totally devoted to him.

We are the ones who cannot see the difference between distraction and devotion, and so we do things to prove our devotion even though Jesus keeps on telling us that the proof is in our hearts, not in the things we do.

The apostle Paul says we should engage in spiritual disciplines in order to train ourselves, like athletes, to adhere to the customs and manners of the kingdom of heaven. They also help us maintain a single-minded focus on the king we now serve (1 Corinthians 9:23-27).

Spiritual disciplines prepare us for the challenges we will face. Often, the "spirit is willing, but the flesh is weak" (Matthew 26:41b). The disciplines remind us, that is, they remind our flesh, that it has no rights of its own. We are controlled by God's will and we will not even let our own bodies diminish our allegiance and obedience to Jesus. We remain relentlessly obedient to Jesus, regardless of how uncomfortable it makes us or the sacrifice it requires.

Jesus takes for granted that his disciples will be involved in inward disciplines such as fasting, meditation, and prayer. They were a normal part of Jesus' life, and so they will become normal to us as the life of Christ emerges from within us.

Fasting is an inward discipline; yet, the self-righteous had turned it outward in an attempt to impress God and impress others. The argument is more or less, "If I show you I am fasting, then I show you I am righteous."

But this is sinful pride and a direct attack on Jesus. If you can do something to prove yourself righteous, then there is no need for Jesus and he can take his bloody crown and chafing cross to someone who really needs it. That's self-righteousness at its core, but we're so used to rationalizing our behaviors and categorizing our sins from the laughable to the egregious that we rarely consider that all self-righteousness is an assault on the cross.

Jesus, perhaps thinking about what it would look like if fasting became an outward discipline, said, "You hypocrites! You clean the outside of your cup and plate, while the inside is full of what you have gotten by violence and selfishness. Blind Pharisee! Clean what is inside the cup first, and then the outside will be clean too" (Matthew 23:25-26).

Ultimately, the disciplines should remind us: From now on, then, you must live the rest of your earthly lives controlled by God's will and not by human desires (1 Peter 4:2). We are led by the Holy Spirit and, as Bonhoeffer notes, "The spirit knows the right way, and desires to follow it, but the flesh lacks courage and finds it too hard, too hazardous and wearisome, and so it stifles the voice of the spirit."

We are called to live the life of Christ in our flesh and blood and the disciplines help us to subjugate our own desires when Jesus calls us to a higher standard. "The spirit assents when Jesus bids us love our enemies," says Bonhoeffer, "but flesh and blood are too strong and prevent our carrying it out."

He adds, "When all is said and done, the life of faith is nothing if not an unending struggle of the spirit with every available weapon against the flesh. How is it possible to live the life of faith when we grow weary of prayer, when we lose our taste for reading the Bible, and when sleep, food and sensuality deprive us of the joy of communion with God?"

⁓

### The Cost of Discipleship—

We must admit that our own undisciplined natures cause as many problems as much as the devil. "I harden my body with blows and bring it under complete control, to keep myself from being disqualified after having called others to the contest" (1 Corinthians 9:27).

### Fallen Thinking—

- I will seek the praise of others above all else, and show them how righteously I live. God may provide for some of my needs, but I don't trust him to see my efforts to seek him, and I don't trust him to bring me the praise of others.
- I must show people how devoted I am to God and how godly I am.

### Kingdom Thinking—

- The disciplines remind me that I must live the rest of my earthly life controlled by God's will and not by my human desires (1 Peter 4:2).

- I will seek the Kingdom of God above all else, and live righteously through my union with Christ, and he will give me everything I need (based on Matthew 6:33 NLT).

## Your Choice?

"Steep your life in God-reality, God-initiative, God-provisions. Don't worry about missing out. You'll find all your everyday human concerns will be met." (Matthew 6:33 MSG) Will you steep your life in God-reality, God-initiative, God-provisions or not?

# 17

## BECOMING LIKE JESUS IN TRUSTING THE FATHER

*"The life of discipleship can only be maintained so long as
nothing is allowed to come between Christ and ourselves—
neither the law, nor personal piety, nor even the world."*

DIETRICH BONHOEFFER

*Do not store up riches for yourselves here on earth, where moths and
rust destroy, and robbers break in and steal. Instead, store up riches for
yourselves in heaven, where moths and rust cannot destroy, and robbers
cannot break in and steal. For your heart will always be where your
riches are.*

*The eyes are like a lamp for the body. If your eyes are sound, your whole
body will be full of light; but if your eyes are no good, your body will be in
darkness. So if the light in you is darkness, how terribly dark it will be!*

*You cannot be a slave of two masters; you will hate one and love the
other; you will be loyal to one and despise the other. You cannot serve both
God and money.*

MATTHEW 6:19-24

Jesus' Objective—*To teach us that our worry reveals the
places where we are not obediently trusting Jesus.*

The secret to carefree living is to stay focused on Jesus, always looking to him
for direction and provision. If you look anywhere else, you're simply setting
yourself up for worry and eventual failure. Jesus is the rock we build our lives
upon; anything else is simply sinking sand.

Bonhoeffer says when we focus on anything other than Jesus, we are looking at a mirage of the real world. We're simply trafficking in shadows that shift and slip away without warning. By focusing on Christ, we catch a glimpse of the real world established in the kingdom of heaven.

We are disciples because we keep our focus singular, on Jesus—never Jesus-plus-the-law, Jesus-plus-religion, Jesus-plus-the-world. Our inability to remain focused exclusively on Christ is at the crux of why we have such difficulty living carefree within the grace of God. It is why we struggle to find the abundant life promised by Jesus and why we have such difficulty resting in the arms of God, wiggling ourselves with child-like faith into the Sabbath rest promised by God.

When we live out our faith as if we're to adhere to Jesus-plus-the-law or Jesus-plus-proving-we're-nice-people, then we are submitting ourselves to two masters—and Jesus says that will never work. We will end up hating one and loving the other.

The point is, we've already established a pattern where we are in revolt against God. *Surely there must be more to the gospel than following Jesus in faith. Surely I must do something.* And, in our desperate attempts to create heaven on earth, it's not much of a walk from the intersection of Jesus-plus-the-extra-things-I-must-do-to-please-God to the intersection of Jesus-plus-a-better-salary-will-make-my-life-complete.

Both are attempts to earn our way into the kingdom of heaven; both are flagrant statements that Jesus is not adequate and that our security lies in our own efforts as much as it does in Jesus, the Mediator between God and man. The *alleged* Mediator is really what we're saying.

This all serves to create a version of Christianity that is an add-on to the good life we all chase. Life with Jesus; going to church; helping other people: it's all part of a value added package. Rather than defining our lives, Jesus is simply a part of our lives.

But Jesus will have none of that. Bonhoeffer explains, "Our hearts have room only for one all-embracing devotion, and we can only cleave to one Lord. Every competitor to that devotion must be hated. As Jesus says, there is no alternative—either we love God or we hate him."

We are quick to argue that is not the case—of course, we are wholeheartedly devoted to Jesus—but then we try to combine our love for him with love for something else: Jesus-plus-a-nice-house; Jesus-plus-that-promotion-at-work; Jesus-plus-a-dental-plan; Jesus-plus-the-latest-fashion-trend.

We end up in a struggle to remain loyal to Jesus while also allowing a loyalty for things like possessions, promotions, praise and pleasure—this shadow life—to creep into our hearts. Trying to be devoted to these two masters is so unnatural that it causes the excessive stress characteristic of twenty-first century living.

We wonder why our lives are filled with anxiety and worry and selfishness, never seeing these things as symptoms of faithlessness. We look out for #1 because we believe no one else—not even Jesus—is looking out for us, and so we have to do it ourselves.

## OUR POSSESSIONS REVEAL OUR TRUE DEVOTION

Jesus says our possessions, or the things that possess us, expose what we are devoted to; they reveal where our heart lies. Bonhoeffer notes Jesus isn't suggesting that to be a Christian means you must live in poverty; rather, he's talking about possessions that posses you. Are you prepared to give it away when asked or, like the rich young man, will you walk away saddened because you are possessed by much.

God gives us possessions (really, we're just stewards) not so we can hoard them, but so we can use them to bring him glory and advance his kingdom. In the wilderness, God gave the Hebrews manna to sustain them, but it spoiled when they tried to hoard it. God also provides for the disciple every *day*, and if the disciple builds bigger barns to preserve the wealth, he ruins not only the wealth but himself as well. Jesus warns that our hearts are devoted to what we treasure. When material 'worship' of material wealth works its way into our hearts, it becomes a barrier that separates us from Christ and the Father.

When we hoard, we are running counter to the trusting, faith-filled culture found in the kingdom of heaven. When we hoard, we are declaring God is not our provider or protector. When we hoard, we are saying something other than God provides for our security, and believing that reveals we are hopelessly lost in the idolatrous thinking of this world.

Our security comes from God. Hoarding is idolatry. Dietrich Bonhoeffer says, "Where our treasure is, there is our trust, our security, our consolation and our God."

We close our hearts to Jesus from fear our possessions will be lost by following him further down the path toward the kingdom of heaven. We undermine life together by stuffing our garages and storage units with things we could be giving to others—and we do this in case we have a need in the future. Why not trust God when the need arises?

Does this mean we can't have some savings, or buy extra light bulbs? You have to ask Jesus that question and that's the point. We gather and collect without ever asking Jesus what we should do, or why he is providing more than we need. Perhaps it is for a future need, or perhaps it is to give away.

"The way to misuse our possessions is to use them as an insurance against the morrow," says Bonhoeffer. "Anxiety is always directed to the morrow, whereas goods are in the strictest sense meant to be used only for today. By trying to ensure for the next day we are only creating uncertainty today."

How do we know the difference between the things we need to keep for legitimate use and those that represent an unnecessary accumulation of possessions?

Bonhoeffer says we only need reverse the words of Jesus: the place you will most want to be, and end up being, is the place where your treasure is. Small or large, Bonhoeffer says, "Everything which hinders us from loving God above all things and acts as a barrier between ourselves and our obedience to Jesus is our treasure, and the place where our heart is."

Yet, "Jesus does not deprive the human heart of its instinctive needs—treasure, glory and praise," says Bonhoeffer. "But he gives it higher objects —the glory of God (John 5.44), the glorying in the cross (Gal. 6.14), and the treasure in heaven."

> This is why I tell you: do not be worried about the food and drink you need in order to stay alive, or about clothes for your body. After all, isn't life worth more than food? And isn't the body worth more than clothes?
>
> Look at the birds: they do not plant seeds, gather a harvest and put it in barns; yet your Father in heaven takes care of them! Aren't you worth much more than birds? Can any of you live a bit longer by worrying about it?
>
> And why worry about clothes? Look how the wild flowers grow: they do not work or make clothes for themselves. But I tell you that not even King Solomon with all his wealth had clothes as beautiful as one of these flowers. It is God

*who clothes the wild grass—grass that is here today and gone tomorrow,*
*burned up in the oven. Won't he be all the more sure to clothe you? What little*
*faith you have!*

*So do not start worrying: 'Where will my food come from? or my drink? or*
*my clothes?' (These are the things the pagans are always concerned about.)*
*Your Father in heaven knows that you need all these things. Instead, be*
*concerned above everything else with the Kingdom of God and with what he*
*requires of you, and he will provide you with all these other things. So do not*
*worry about tomorrow; it will have enough worries of its own. There is no*
*need to add to the troubles each day brings. Matthew 6:25-34*

## SERVING THINGS INSTEAD OF JESUS

The more we possess, the more we have to care for our possessions and that
leads to our possessions eventually possessing us. Jesus doesn't forbid us to
have possessions. His point is that we should not allow our possessions to get
in the way of following him—and the more we accumulate, the more likely we
are to worry about how we will pay for, take care of, keep and protect the things
we own.

Bonhoeffer notes, "If our hearts are set on them, our reward is an anxiety
whose burden is intolerable. Anxiety creates its own treasures and they in turn
beget further care." It leads to a cycle of always putting off our total abandonment to Jesus. We think, "When I get this much in the bank, then I'll focus more
on ministry. If I could just get a bigger house, then I'll be able to host a small
group in my home."

And that leads to scenarios where we are unable to respond to Jesus because
we're weighted down with worry and regret and too much stuff. We're unable
to volunteer—that is, do the ministry Jesus calls us to do—because we have to
work extra hours to pay for the things we have. We sense Jesus telling us to step
out in faith to pursue a different career, one that matches the way he has shaped
us for ministry—but then we think, "I can't quit my job, Jesus, I have a mort-
gage to pay."

Jesus drives deep into the heart of our thinking, where we load ourselves down
with obligations he never intended for us to carry and that creates worry that
distracts us from following him faithfully. We can't do what he's told us to do

simply because we have too many other things we have to do in order to take care of the things we have.

Suddenly, we're serving things instead of serving Jesus. We begin to believe, "It is all up to me to pay for these things and to provide for my needs and my family's needs." And that is fallen thinking locked into the economy of this world. Jesus says in God's economy, in the kingdom of heaven, our Father is the provider and he knows our needs better than we do ourselves. *Look around, look at how he provides. Now believe he will provide for you.*

Bonhoeffer says, "It is senseless to pretend that we can make provision because we cannot alter the circumstances of this world. Only God can take care, for it is he who rules the world. Since we cannot take care, since we are so completely powerless, we ought not to do it either. If we do, we are dethroning God and presuming to rule the world ourselves."

We cannot even predict what will happen tomorrow, which reveals our arrogance at believing in our own ability to provide over God's ability to see and meet our needs. We grasp for what we can see rather than being faithful to the unseen Father who Jesus says cares for us deeply. We—petty, little lords incapable of controlling the future or even our present circumstances—demand control even though the Creator and Master of the universe stands ready to fulfill our every need.

The cost of discipleship is giving up this control and our insistence on maintaining control keeps us *too large* to enter through the narrow gate into the kingdom of heaven. The sign that we are still grabbing for control is worry. When we worry, we reveal our lack of faith. Jesus, again, brings us to a choice.

Will you trust me or will you not trust me? If you trust me, you will not worry; if you worry, then you do not trust me.

We think, *But . . . but . . . but . . .*. Jesus gives no wiggle room on worry. When we worry, we have stopped following Jesus. When we worry, we are no longer submitted to Jesus. When we worry, we sin. Jesus went to the cross because of our worry; yet, it is an overwhelmingly accepted sin within the Christian community.

Bonhoeffer notes that the birds and the lilies "glorify their Creator, not by their industry, toil or care, but by a daily unquestioning acceptance of his gifts." A characteristic of fallen thinking is that there is a "cause and effect between work and sustenance, but Jesus explodes that illusion. According to him, bread is not to be valued as the reward for work; he speaks instead of the carefree simplicity of the man who walks with him and accepts everything as it comes from God."

## EVERYTHING COMES FROM GOD

To echo Martin Luther, "Who put the food that the birds will find where they could find it?" This drives us deeper into kingdom thinking. Jesus topples the mythology that what you do is a measure of what you are worth, which is just another variation on the mythology of earning your way into God's good graces. This is one way we cheapen grace because we say the work of Jesus provides for our salvation, but it doesn't have anything to do with our survival or sustenance here on earth.

Jesus says anxiety is characteristic of the pagans (those who do not believe in God, but consider also those who do not have *faith* in God). "They do not know that the Father knows that we have need of all these things, and so they try to do for themselves what they do not expect from God," says Bonhoeffer.

How many of us are practicing pagans, as troubled by worry and fear as an infested dog is troubled by fleas? As we follow Jesus we will see that we lack nothing that we need. The issue, then, is not *if* God can be trusted; the issue is with our ability to trust.

How would our churches change if we made it absolutely understandable that worry is a sin? How would our Christ-communities change if we preached and taught "Do not worry"—and said, "We're going to keep working on this every week until we're all safe and mature in the words of Christ?"

How would your life change if you asked God to teach you not to worry—and you said, "God, keep me focused on this until I finally obediently trust you." To not worry means you trust Jesus. He is for you, not against you. He wants you to learn to obediently trust him: "Do not let your hearts be troubled. Trust in God; trust also in me." (John 14:1 NIV)

### The Cost of Discipleship—

We must give away our worry in exchange for trusting God. "The Lord's unfailing love and mercy still continue, Fresh as the morning, as sure as the sunrise. The Lord is all I have, and so in him I put my hope." (Lamentations 3:22-24)

### Fallen Thinking—

- I'm worried about this because who else will take care of it? Besides, the more I worry, the more the situation is resolved. Worry even puts money in my bank account.
- I'd better get as many of these as I can or I will have to go without. I'd better take this great deal now. Even God couldn't provide this for me at a better price.
- Oh, by the way, Jesus, I needed a new (item) so I bought it. I guess I should have asked you about it first, but it's not like you'd provide it for me some other way. I mean, that's what *my* money is for, right?

### Kingdom Thinking—

- My worry is a signal, not to try harder, but to trust more.
- I am worried about this. Jesus, show me why I am not trusting you with this particular situation.
- I feel like I have to buy more of these and stockpile them. Jesus, help me to remember how you have provided for me every time I needed something.
- Jesus, I need this (item) and I know you are aware of my need. Should I purchase it or will you provide it in another way?

### Your Choice?

Will you obediently trust Jesus or will you put more faith in your worry? Do you believe things would be different if you put as much time into prayer as you do worry? If yes, why don't you do just that?

# 18

## BECOMING LIKE JESUS IN OUR ACCEPTANCE OF NON-BELIEVERS

*"How easy it would have been for the disciples to adopt a superior attitude, to pass unqualified condemnation on the rest of the world, and to persuade themselves that this was the will of God!"*

DIETRICH BONHOEFFER

*Do not judge others, so that God will not judge you, for God will judge you in the same way you judge others, and he will apply to you the same rules you apply to others. Why, then, do you look at the speck in your brother's eye and pay no attention to the log in your own eye? How dare you say to your brother, 'Please, let me take that speck out of your eye,' when you have a log in your own eye? You hypocrite! First take the log out of your own eye, and then you will be able to see clearly to take the speck out of your brother's eye.*

*"Do not give what is holy to dogs—they will only turn and attack you. Do not throw your pearls in front of pigs—they will only trample them underfoot."*

*Ask, and you will receive; seek, and you will find; knock, and the door will be opened to you. For everyone who asks will receive, and anyone who seeks will find, and the door will be opened to those who knock. Would any of you who are fathers give your son a stone when he asks for bread? Or would you give him a snake when he asks for a fish? As bad as you are, you know how to give good things to your children. How much more, then, will your Father in heaven give good things to those who ask him!*

*Do for others what you want them to do for you: this is the meaning of the Law of Moses and of the teachings of the prophets.*

MATTHEW 7:1-12

*Jesus' Objective—To teach us that seeing what God sees*
*in others is more important and helpful than judging*
*them according to appearance or performance.*

Like Joshua at the borders of the Promised Land, Jesus brings us to where we can see the kingdom of heaven spread out before us. We must separate from our old life, and the boundaries between the old and new are very clear.

But Bonhoeffer says this raises the question of how we should relate to our non-Christian neighbors. One thing is clear, there is no room for harsh judgment because the source of our new life lies exclusively in our fellowship with Jesus Christ. Our righteousness comes only from our union with Jesus and not from anything we've done, not from anything outside of our relationship with him.

For that very reason, says Bonheoffer, we can never use our righteousness as a measurement applied against the life of others, in particular those who are not in union with Christ. We have not set the standard for Christian living; rather, we follow Jesus Christ, the Mediator and very Son of God, who applies his righteousness to us.

With this in mind, we have no justification for maintaining a superior, judgmental, *holier-than-thou* view over anyone. *There but for the grace of God go I.* It is not our place to tell others how they ought to live; rather, our role is to take them to Jesus and he can tell them how to find life, a life extraordinary.

Bonhoeffer says, "It is not an approved standard of righteous living that separates a follower of Christ from the unbeliever, but it is Christ who stands between them. Christians always see other men as brethren to whom Christ comes; they meet them only by going to them with Jesus."

## WE SEE PEOPLE DIFFERENTLY

Because we belong to Jesus, we can no longer judge others independent of Jesus. We must see them through the eyes of Jesus. "No longer, then, do we judge anyone by human standards," says the apostle Paul. "Even if at one time we judged Christ according to human standards, we no longer do so. Anyone who is joined to Christ is a new being; the old is gone, the new has come."

Paul adds, "All this is done by God, who through Christ changed us from enemies into his friends and gave us the task of making others his friends also. Our message is that God was making all human beings his friends through Christ. God did not keep an account of their sins, and he has given us the message which tells how he makes them his friends" (2 Corinthians 5:16-18).

We cannot even look at ourselves in a detached way, as if we can judge ourselves to be good or bad independent of Jesus. Jesus says we only fool ourselves when we become certain of our own goodness. It's a devilish thinking that leads us to look down on everybody else. Jesus once told this story—

"Once there were two men who went up to the Temple to pray: one was a Pharisee, the other a tax collector. The Pharisee stood apart by himself and prayed, 'I thank you, God, that I am not greedy, dishonest, or an adulterer, like everybody else. I thank you that I am not like that tax collector over there. I fast two days a week, and I give you one tenth of all my income.'"

"But the tax collector stood at a distance and would not even raise his face to heaven, but beat on his breast and said, 'God, have pity on me, a sinner!' I tell you," said Jesus, "the tax collector, and not the Pharisee, was in the right with God when he went home. For those who make themselves great will be humbled, and those who humble themselves will be made great" (Luke 18:10-14).

## GOD SHOWS US THEIR FAULTS SO WE WILL PRAY

Bonhoeffer says, "Here alone Christ's fight for the soul of the unbeliever, his call, his love, his grace and his judgement comes into its own. Discipleship does not afford us a point of vantage from which to attack others; we come to them with an unconditional offer of fellowship, with the single-mindedness of the love of Jesus."

Oswald Chambers says in *My Utmost for His Highest*: "When we discern that other people are not growing spiritually and allow that discernment to turn to criticism, we block our fellowship with God. God never gives us discernment so that we may criticize, but that we may intercede."[11]

The discernment God gives us is meant to push us toward the other-centered position of prayer and support in the Spirit of "love, joy, peace, patience, kindness, goodness, faithfulness, gentleness and self-control" (Galatians 5:22–23 NIV).

Since we are in union with Christ, Bonhoeffer says unbelievers now have a claim upon our love. We no longer have the choice to say, "They did this to themselves." We are called to bear their sins, to bear their pain and, like Jesus, see the endgame with a desire to bring them into the kingdom of heaven.

Bonhoeffer says, "I am not forbidden to have my own thoughts about the other person, to realize his shortcomings, but only to the extent that it offers to me an occasion for forgiveness and unconditional love . . . ." Withholding judgment doesn't condone the other person's sin or confirm the other person's bad ways.

## LOVE, NOT JUDGMENT, CONDEMNS SIN

The unconditional love of Jesus flowing through us will condemn their sins far better than anything we could do or say and the Holy Spirit working on them will convict them for their sin. The issue is, will we trust God to handle judgment or will we insist on bringing our own judgment into the relationship?

This doesn't mean Jesus is telling us to take a laissez-faire attitude toward sin. Jesus is very aware of the cost of sin; rather, we need to respond to sin in the manner Jesus tells us to, not according to our own desires.

In addition, Jesus is not suggesting Christians cannot oppose wrong thinking in the church. In his commentary on Matthew, John MacArthur notes the command not to judge does not mean we cannot confront a brother or sister slipping into sin. Jesus clearly calls us to do that. MacArthur says we have the "right to oppose wrong doctrine or wrong practices in the church." This is important to understand, he says, because, "if we are afraid to confront falsehood and sin in the church, we will be inclined to become undiscriminating and undiscerning. The church, and our own lives, will become more and more in danger of corruption."[12]

But that doesn't excuse us from loving those we confront with unconditional love. By loving them without condition, we pull them out of the balance sheet mentality we have in this world, where we think the bad we do must be counter-balanced with good.

"Neither I am right nor the other person, but God is always right and shall proclaim both his grace and his judgement," Bonhoeffer says. We are to love the sinner unconditionally and "the love of Christ for the sinner in itself is the condemnation of sin, is his expression of extreme hatred of sin."

But when we judge other people, Bonhoeffer says we force them onto the balance sheet of good and evil. We're back thinking like fallen humans who broke communion with God in order to gain the knowledge of good and evil. If we judge evil in others and think that should count against them, then that also means we must judge good in them and that must count for them. And so, we put them in the very cycle Jesus came to end, where they have to do more good than evil in order to be acceptable to God.

But, first, they must be acceptable to us because we have supplanted God in his sovereignty to decide how he will handle evil, revenge, and justice. Our judgment is nothing less than the undermining of the work of Jesus on the cross.

The problem is, when we put others into this cycle of judgment, we also drag ourselves back into it. Our good deeds must now be measured against our evil deeds because the same standards apply to everyone. We have not earned our righteousness and so we're in no position to insist others earn theirs. To do so is nothing short of heretical; it is a re-writing of the gospels for our own self-ish motives, meant to benefit ourselves and those we deem acceptable and to punish those we deem as unacceptable or irresponsible or just too obnoxious to be worthy of God's unconditional love. It is a declaration by us that they are unworthy and irredeemable but our judgment sets us up as little gods and that brings God's judgment on us.

Bonheoffer says if our motive is to root out evil, then we must start with the evil in ourselves instead of being the blind ophthalmologists that Jesus describes, who try to fix the flawed vision in others even though their ability to see into the kingdom of heaven is completely blocked by their own super-sized judgment.

Perhaps it is no coincidence that the people who are most judgmental tend to be the people who are legalistic about keeping a balance sheet of good and evil. Bonhoeffer notes, "To everyone God is the kind of God he believes in."

Our behavior exposes our beliefs and, if you believe in a God who demands a balance sheet, then you'll be a zealot to keep one. At the same time, if you believe in a God who willingly lowers his standards of holiness and righteousness to meet your human imperfections, then you'll continue to live as if free grace means cheap grace.

"Judging others makes us blind," says Bonheoffer, "whereas love is illuminating. By judging others we blind ourselves to our own evil and to the grace which others are just as entitled to as we are."

It is only by seeing with the eyes of Christ, as we look at others from the foot of the cross, that we are able to see them with clarity, understanding *they need forgiveness in the same way we do*. The changing of our perspective on this is one marker of our passage from this world into the kingdom of heaven.

Bonhoeffer notes when we judge others we depersonalize them. They're no longer flesh and blood beings in need of Jesus. They become our *faux cross* to bear because of their annoyances.

## CAN WE JUDGE OUR ENEMIES?

But Jesus does not limit those we cannot judge to the familiar. He tells us not to judge any human being because all humans are created in the image of God. When we objectify and dehumanize our enemies, using the common racial slurs, we undermine our own ability to love them unconditionally—which is what Jesus commands us to do.

Jesus does not give us the power or the right to force the gospel on others. This is why we waste our time when we demand non-believers to act as if they believe. He says we are casting pearls before swine. This is also why we waste our time trying to legislate Christianity. Jesus never suggests a nation can become Christian by legislation or imperial command.

When we try to force others to believe in Jesus, we deny the power of Christ to persuade men through his unconditional love. We deny the power of his death and resurrection to transform lives. Jesus doesn't need us to force people to change. He is perfectly capable of bringing about change in their lives; our role is to obediently trust Jesus will use his life flowing through us to nudge people toward change. It requires faith to believe Jesus will transform the lives of others and the cost of discipleship for us is to get out of the way as he works through us.

On the other hand, Bonhoeffer says, "Our easy trafficking with the word of cheap grace simply bores the world to disgust, so that in the end it turns against those who try to force on it what it does not want."

In other words, even the fallen world can see when we lower the standards of our faith and they scorn us for our compromise. And lest anyone rush to judgment, lowering the standards of costly grace isn't limited to moral compromise or marketing an easy gospel where we seemingly reduce the responsibility of a believer. The legalist is just as guilty of compromise—a watered-down gospel—when he reduces the life of Christ flowing through us to a list of rules: and the politically inclined ignores the transformational power of grace when she tries to legislate the kind of behavior that can only emerge from someone who has the life of Jesus planted deep in his heart.

Jesus says when we encounter opposition, rather than forcing beliefs on others, we should simply shake the dust off our feet and move along. We do not have to win the argument. Jesus has already won and, if the power of his call is not enough to persuade men and women to his side, he certainly doesn't need us pleading with others to follow.

Bonhoeffer notes Jesus limits our activity. We are no longer responsible for those people. We can shake the dust from our feet and move on. Bonhoeffer notes, within the vast scope of the Great Commission, Jesus limits our activity. We are no longer responsible for those people and in that, we are reminded that our activity is limited to exactly what Jesus tells us to do.

The thing is, Bonhoeffer says, Jesus is willing to risk the scorn and rejection of others. With "divine humility," he's not afraid to appear weak, not afraid that the gospel may appear weak. "The same weak Word which is content to endure the gainsaying of sinners is also the mighty Word of mercy which can convert the hearts of sinners," says Bonhoeffer. "Its strength is veiled in weakness; if it came in power that would mean that the day of judgement had arrived."

The disciples do not possess any rights or powers over others that come to them independent of Jesus and so they have absolutely no justification for lording the righteousness *they have been given* over others.

The disciples can only reach others *for Jesus through Jesus*. We should stop being so impressed with those who carry the anointing of God and instead be impressed by the God who is able to anoint those of his choosing.

The disciples are taught to pray and in that develop the humility of knowing they can only reach others by praying to God. The disciples are told "judgment and forgiveness are always in the hands of God" (Bonhoeffer). Jesus opens and closes the hearts and minds of men, not our persuasive abilities and not our strength—and certainly not our judgment.

### The Cost of Discipleship—

Jesus teaches us that seeing what God sees in others is more important and helpful than judging them according to appearance or performance. We must begin moving from self-centeredness to other-centeredness, where we do for others what we want them to do for us.

### Fallen Thinking—

- Why should I have to pay the unfair price so that others go free?
- I should point out all their faults so they can agree with me and that will change them

### Kingdom Thinking—

- How can I minister to the needs of others rather than trying to manipulate their behavior?
- Jesus, what do you want me to do to address the needs behind this person's flaws?
- This person is in need of Jesus, just as I am.

### Your Choice?

The life of Jesus flows from him into us, transforming us. We have no basis for judging others; in fact, we must now see them as Jesus see them—with compassion and love. Knowing this, will you continue to judge others or will you allow the love of God to flow through you to them?

# 19

## Becoming Like Jesus in Abandonment

*"The path of discipleship is narrow, and it is fatally easy to miss one's way and stray from the path, even after years of discipleship. And it is hard to find. On either side of the narrow path deep chasms yawn."*

Dietrich Bonhoeffer

*Go in through the narrow gate, because the gate to hell is wide and the road that leads to it is easy, and there are many who travel it. But the gate to life is narrow and the way that leads to it is hard, and there are few people who find it.*

*Be on your guard against false prophets; they come to you looking like sheep on the outside, but on the inside they are really like wild wolves.*

*You will know them by what they do. Thorn bushes do not bear grapes, and briers do not bear figs. A healthy tree bears good fruit, but a poor tree bears bad fruit. A healthy tree cannot bear bad fruit, and a poor tree cannot bear good fruit. And any tree that does not bear good fruit is cut down and thrown in the fire.*

*So then, you will know the false prophets by what they do. Not everyone who calls me 'Lord, Lord' will enter the Kingdom of heaven, but only those who do what my Father in heaven wants them to do. When the Judgment Day comes, many will say to me, 'Lord, Lord! In your name we spoke God's message, by your name we drove out many demons and performed many miracles!' Then I will say to them, 'I never knew you. Get away from me, you wicked people!'*

Matthew 7:13-23

*Jesus' Objective—To teach us that the fruit we bear
comes from the life of Christ working within us.*

J esus never said our journey into the kingdom of heaven would be easy and
    we won't get there on good intentions. It is, after all, the road to hell and not
the road to heaven that is paved with good intentions. Only the life of Christ
working within us will give us the Jesus shape we need to fit through the narrow gate.

We must abandon ourselves to the life of Christ that is at work, producing
in us, not only the character of Jesus, but also the fruit of a life lived submitted
to God.

Bonhoeffer reiterates that it is only when we are abandoned to Christ that we
are able to live the life of Christ:

> To be called to a life of extraordinary quality, to live up to it, and yet
> to be unconscious of it, is indeed a narrow way.
>
> To confess and testify to the truth as it is in Jesus, and at the same
> time to love the enemies of that truth, his enemies and ours, and to love
> them with the infinite love of Jesus Christ, is indeed a narrow way.
>
> To believe the promise of Jesus that his followers shall possess
> the earth, and at the same time to face our enemies unarmed and
> defenseless, preferring to incur injustice rather than to do wrong
> ourselves, is indeed a narrow way.
>
> To see the weakness and wrong in others, and at the same time
> refrain from judging them; to deliver the gospel message without
> casting pearls before swine, is indeed a narrow way.

Jesus says we are like vines that run off his branch. As long as we are connected to him, we bear fruit (John 15). Without him, we cannot bear fruit. Without
him, we are, at best, people trying to live moral lives, but without a connection
to the source of right living. We may appear to be godly, but, in truth, we deny
the power of God in our lives.

When we try to do ministry independent from Jesus, we deny the power of
God in our lives. We may do things that are noble and require considerable

sacrifice, but if they are done independent from Jesus, then they are done outside the will of God. That is sin.

Our authority to do things in the name of Jesus only comes from our obedient trust of Jesus. Otherwise, how can we say we come in his name? The Word of God says we can do all things through Jesus, but we can do nothing apart from Jesus. There is no middle ground. We either do it with Jesus, or what we do amounts to nothing in the kingdom of heaven. We are either dependent upon Jesus or we are independent of him.

You may call this a radical faith; some may call this a radical Christology, but in the kingdom of heaven it is perfectly normal. And that's why in this world's kingdom it is considered revolutionary thinking.

"There is nothing in us that allows us to claim that we are capable of doing this work," Paul says. "The capacity we have comes from God; it is he who made us capable of serving the new covenant, which consists not of a written law but of the Spirit. The written law brings death, but the Spirit gives life" (2 Corinthians 3:5-6).

The very narrowness of the road increases our need to rely upon Jesus. "The way which the Son of God trod on earth, and the way which we too must tread as citizens of two worlds on the razor edge between this world and the kingdom of heaven, could hardly be a broad way," says Bonhoeffer (For this reason, he adds, we should never hang our hopes on huge numbers).

Like a man who survives a heart attack, Jesus gives us new life but, like a man who survives a heart attack, we must now learn to live an entirely different way than we have before. We must *abandon* the bad behaviors and unhealthy habits that brought us to death.

Jesus warns us that there will be those who come, appearing as his servants, yet with the intent of pulling us away from the intentions of God. They will want to focus us on their agenda—and their agenda may even appear good, but if it pulls us away from Jesus, then the truth is they are evil.

There is no middle ground. We either become flush with the intentions of God or we remain uneven with them. And that is often why we experience a rough time, not because things are particularly hard, or because we are suffering for our faith, but because we are uneven with the intentions of God.

Jesus says these false prophets will not be easy to spot. They may look like Christians and talk like Christians—they may even act better than most

Christians, appearing to be the most pious among us. "After all, other men's hearts are always a closed book," explains Bonhoeffer. "Thus [the false prophet] succeeds in seducing many from the [narrow path]. He may even be unconscious himself of what he is doing."

The only way to spot these false prophets, Jesus says, is by their fruit. "Sooner or later we shall find out where a man stands," Bonhoeffer notes. "It is no use the tree refusing to bear any fruit, for the fruit comes of its own accord." We bear fruit in intimacy with Jesus, never without. "I am the vine, and you are the branches," says Jesus. "Those who remain in me, and I in them, will bear much fruit; for you can do nothing without me" (John 15:5).

Jesus continues to declare that Christianity is not a religion of appearances. We are called to a relationship, not a code of ethics, and we are called to an authentic relationship, one that is true and transparent. Jesus knows our heart and his aim is to strip away any murky mythology that keeps us from being exactly what we are called to be, which is 'what you see is what you get' believers.

We chase Jesus, not the rules. We chase after his heart, not mere forgiveness. We abandon to the life of Christ within us and we watch what fruit we bear. As a result, Bonhoeffer says, "At any moment the nominal Christians may be separated from the real ones. We may even find that we are nominal Christians ourselves. [This is our] challenge to closer fellowship with Jesus and to a more loyal discipleship."

A mere confession of Christ is not enough, Bonhoeffer notes. "God will not ask us in that day whether we were good Protestants, but whether we have done his will."

As Jesus explained to Martha, we need not be worried and troubled over so many things because just one thing is needed—to remain intimate with him (Luke 10:41-42). And by this, we work within the realm of costly grace, understanding it is not our right to be there, but that we are there because of the bloody work and blessed resurrection of Jesus.

We come to him in this humility and we serve him with this humility. There is no place in the kingdom of heaven for self-righteousness and, in the end, Jesus says he will be unmerciful to those who insist the fruit they bear on their own is fit for the kingdom of heaven. Those who say, "Look at what I've done for you," will hear Jesus say, "I never knew you."

Bonhoeffer says, "At this point Jesus reveals to his disciples the possibility of a demonic faith which produces wonderful works quite indistinguishable from the works of the true disciples, works of charity, miracles, perhaps even of personal sanctification, but which is nevertheless a denial of Jesus and of the life of discipleship."

What is required of us, in the end, is intimacy with Jesus, the Incarnate Word of God. There can be no competition between us and Jesus. We are called to be a picture of Jesus, never of ourselves. Our discipleship is built on one person, the Lord Jesus Christ.

"The end of the Sermon on the Mount echoes the beginning," says Bonhoeffer. "The word of the last judgement is foreshadowed in the call to discipleship. But from beginning to end it is always his word and his call, his alone. If we follow Christ, cling to his word, and let everything else go, it will see us through the day of judgement. His word is his grace."

## The Cost of Discipleship—
Jesus says it is not enough to just do; we must do within our intimate connection to him. He doesn't want us running off to save the world for him; he wants us to abide in him and bear the fruit he nurtures in us.

## Fallen Thinking—
- I can try harder and become more like Jesus.
- My fruit is dependent upon the context, not the content of my life.

## Kingdom Thinking—
- I cannot grow my own fruit, but I can anticipate the fruit of a Christ-centered life.
- Fruit is borne and I consent to allowing Jesus Christ to be himself in and through me.

### Your Choice?

Will you try harder to bear fruit, or will you trust Jesus to bear fruit through you? Will you abandon to the life of Christ working within you, or will you analyze according to what you can see?

# 20

## BECOMING LIKE JESUS IN WISDOM

*"We have listened to the Sermon on the Mount and perhaps have understood
it. But who has heard it aright? Jesus gives the answer at the end. He does not
allow his hearers to go away and make of his sayings what they will, picking and
choosing from them whatever they find helpful, and testing them to see if they work."*

DIETRICH BONHOEFFER

*So then, anyone who hears these words of mine and obeys them is like a wise
man who built his house on rock. The rain poured down, the rivers flooded
over, and the wind blew hard against that house. But it did not fall, because
it was built on rock.*

*But anyone who hears these words of mine and does not obey them is like
a foolish man who built his house on sand. The rain poured down, the rivers
flooded over, the wind blew hard against that house, and it fell. And what a
terrible fall that was!*

*When Jesus finished saying these things, the crowd was amazed at the way
he taught. He wasn't like the teachers of the Law; instead, he taught with
authority.*

MATTHEW 7:24-29

Jesus' Objective—*To teach us that we must* do, *not just* know *God's Word.*

It is not enough to know what we must do, we must do it. Knowing what to do
doesn't count for anything if we never actually do it. In truth, it is disobedience; it is a particularly arrogant form of rebellion, where we hold on to our
right to decide what to do and when to do it.

Jesus says we are to be doers of the word, not just hearers—*anyone who hears and obeys*. The proof of our faith is in the doing. If we obediently believe, then we will build our house on the rock—because we know the storms will inevitably come but we trust Jesus because we believe he knows what he is talking about and so we do what he says—*the crowd was amazed at the way he taught with authority*.

We place our faith in Jesus, God's Word in the flesh and we trust he will make good on all his promises. "The only proper response to this word which Jesus brings with him from eternity is simply to do it," says Bonhoeffer. "Jesus has spoken: his is the word, ours the obedience."

If we don't build our house on the rock, then it means we do not trust Jesus. We do not have faith in him or his promises and so we chose to live faithlessly. "Jesus knows only one possibility: simple surrender and obedience, not interpreting it or applying it, but doing and obeying it," Bonhoeffer says.

There is no other explanation Jesus will accept. When we continue to build our future on the sand, even after hearing the Word of God, then we are in disobedience to Jesus. We reveal we are still stuck in fallen thinking, hedging our bets on what we think may be best, keeping our options open.

Jesus wants us to shut down all the other options and bet it all on him. And the thing is, this is no gamble because he stands on the promises he has made. The issue is not with him; it is with us and our insistence that there must be other options in addition to obeying Jesus.

And if you want to make it through the narrow gate into the kingdom of heaven, that simply isn't true. You are living in a mythological world, a slave to the enemy of God and his fallen thinking: *Why can't you build your house on sand? What does Jesus know about the storms of life? What would a carpenter know about building?*

Surrender to Jesus is hard work and Bonhoeffer suggests our biggest battle is against our own tendency to admire the Sermon on the Mount rather than obey it.

Yet, there is no valid reason for refusing Jesus. In truth, it is in our own best interests to follow him. It is the most practical thing to do, the safest thing to do. The fact that we are so easily convinced that living as a Christian is often impractical reveals how deeply submerged we are in the fallen thinking.

When we think like those who live in the kingdom of heaven, we will know that the most prudent thing we can do is follow Jesus and the most impractical thing is to deny.

And Jesus refuses to coddle us. He offers no middle ground. If you do not obey, you disobey. If you do not live by faith, you live faithlessly. "It is impossible to want to do it and yet not do it," Bonhoeffer says. "To deal with the word of Jesus otherwise than by doing it is to give him the lie. It is to deny the Sermon on the Mount and to say No to his word."

If we know what the Word says, yet do not obey the Word, we are no different from those who do not believe the Word. It does not matter how long and how effectively we argue that this isn't true, the truth remains that when we do not obey, we show we do not believe. The apostle Paul says, "Such people claim they know God, but they deny him by the way they live. They are detestable and disobedient, worthless for doing anything good" (Titus 1:16 NLT).

It is an aspect of cheap grace that we allow this kind of fallen thinking to remain so prevalent in our congregations. Is it any wonder we have so many people in our churches deeply committed to lukewarm commitment to Jesus? If you are not committed to being obedient to Jesus, then where do you land? What would be the middle ground: commitment to passive resistance to Jesus?

We become like the man in the book of James who, after looking in the mirror, forgets what he looks like. "In other words, a person who professes to know Christ but does not obey Christ, has no lasting image of what the new life is all about," says John MacArthur,. "He glimpses Christ, and glimpses what Christ can do for him, but his image of Christ and of the new life in Christ soon fade. His experience with the gospel is shallow, superficial, and short-lived."[13]

We forget who we are and that we are now citizens of the kingdom of heaven and, when we feel so orphaned, we fall back into fallen thinking. James says the man in the mirror is double-mind and that's what we become.

Yet, Jesus, with a rock-solid resolve, adhered to a single-minded obedience to the Father and he calls us to the same single-minded obedience to him. Because Jesus maintained an intimacy with the Father, he taught like one with authority. We are given a similar authority when we remain intimate with Jesus.

The apostle John says, *"And we can be sure that we know him if we obey his commandments. If someone claims, 'I know God,' but doesn't obey God's commandments, that person is a liar and is not living in the truth. But those who obey God's word truly show how completely they love him. That is how we know we are living in him. Those who say they live in God should live their lives as Jesus did"* (1 John 2:6 NLT).

❧

### The Cost of Discipleship—

Instead of trying harder to be like Jesus, we must trust him to be himself in and through us. We must begin to accept the things of the Spirit: "The man without the Spirit does not accept the things that come from the Spirit of God, for they are foolishness to him, and he cannot understand them, because they are spiritually discerned." (1 Corinthians 2:14 NIV)

### Fallen Thinking—

- Stability and security in my life come from my own efforts.
- I must focus on self-improvement, not self-replacement (my 'self' exchanged for the life of Christ working in me).

### Kingdom Thinking—

- Stability and security in my life come from my obedient trust in Jesus (Matt 7:24).
- "This life that I live now, I live by faith in the Son of God, who loved me and gave his life for me" (Galatians 2:20).
- "For what seems to be God's foolishness is wiser than human wisdom, and what seems to be God's weakness is stronger than human strength" (1 Corinthians 1:25).
- We must *do*, not just *know* God's Word. (John 7:17).
- We are blessed by the doing (John 13:17).

### Your Choice?

Will I live by the life of the Son of God in me or will I live as if his life is not present in me? ". . . It is no longer I who live, but it is Christ who lives in me . . . I refuse to reject the grace of God. But if a person is put right with God through the Law, it means that Christ died for nothing!" (Galatians 2:20-21)

# 21

## BECOMING LIKE JESUS IN HIS COMPASSION

*"[Jesus] shrank from the idea of forming an exclusive little coterie with his disciples. Unlike the founders of the great religions, he had no desire to withdraw them from the vulgar crowd and initiate them into an esoteric system of religion and ethics. He had come, he had worked and suffered for the sake of all his people."*

DIETRICH BONHOEFFER

*Jesus went around visiting all the towns and villages. He taught in the synagogues, preached the Good News about the Kingdom, and healed people with every kind of disease and sickness. As he saw the crowds, his heart was filled with pity for them, because they were worried and helpless, like sheep without a shepherd. So he said to his disciples, "The harvest is large, but there are few workers to gather it in. Pray to the owner of the harvest that he will send out workers to gather in his harvest.*

MATTHEW 9:35-38

Jesus' Objective—*To teach us that the life of Christ is given to us to serve others, not just to make us righteous before the Father. We are given the compassion of Christ so we will be compassionate.*

Jesus saw all the harassed and helpless human-sheep and he was moved to extraordinary compassion; the text suggests that it ripped at his guts. Their spiritual leaders—their shepherds—had misused their power and influence in order to meet their own desires instead of serving the people God had sent them to serve.

"No one led the flock to fresh waters to quench their thirst, no one protected them from the wolf," says Bonhoeffer. "They were harassed, wounded and distraught under the dire rod of their shepherds, and lay prostrate upon the ground." Jesus sees people so beaten down by life and facing so many problems, and so overwhelmed, that they don't even know where to go for help (Matthew 9:36).

"There were questions but no answers, distress but no relief, anguish of conscience but no deliverance, tears but no consolation, sin but no forgiveness," says Bonhoeffer. "Where was the good shepherd they needed so badly? What good was it when the scribes herded the people into the schools, when the devotees of the law sternly condemned sinners without lifting a finger to help them? What use were all these orthodox preachers and expounders of the Word, when they were not filled by boundless pity and compassion for God's maltreated and injured people?"

The call of Jesus is not to an isolated ivory tower, where we discuss the meaning of life and try to figure out an intellectual or philosophical approach to Christian ethics. Jesus didn't come to give answers; he is the answer.

He doesn't talk about love; he shows us his love. Jesus works up a sweat; he rolls up his sleeves, gets on his knees, and washes our feet with his blood, sweat, and tears. He waded into the masses, touching them one-by-one. They could look into his eyes, feel his warmth, smell his breath and hear him whisper, "You are healed. I am with you now."

And Jesus proved his promise by healing people with every kind of disease and sickness.

"[The Good Shepherd] knows them all by name and loves them," says Bonhoeffer. "He knows their distress and their weakness. He heals the wounded, gives drink to the thirsty, sets upright the falling, and leads them gently, not sternly, to pasture. He leads them on the right way. He seeks the one lost sheep, and brings it back to the fold."

"But the bad shepherds lord it over the flock by force, forgetting their charges and pursuing their own interests," Bonhoeffer says. "Jesus is looking for good shepherds, and there are none to be found."

Instead, the religious leaders used their power to manipulate and control the masses. Instead of giving, they were taking. As disciples of Jesus, we are called to face-to-face compassion with those in need. He teaches us to help those in need regardless of how we feel about them or what we think about them.

Like Jesus, we empty ourselves, taking on the form of a servant (Philippians 2:7). In serving the "least of these," we show others what Jesus-in-action looks like and, at the same time, we show Jesus that we love him.

Jesus calls us to see others the way he sees them (Ephesians 1:18). He wants to develop in us the same mercy for others that he has and he calls us to become part of God's promise to set the captives free and bring them home to the kingdom of heaven. We will find ourselves—our real lives—by losing ourselves in the lives of others.

Jesus, our master teacher, says, in effect, "I'm not going to keep doing this ministry by myself. I want you to be able to do it too. So, come, work with me and see how the Father fills you with his compassion."

Our service is enabled by God's "mighty power at work within us . . . able to accomplish infinitely more than we would ever dare to ask or hope" (Ephesians 3:20 NLT).

But Jesus also calls us to pray for more workers. There is simply too much work to be done. We must ask God for help; we must remain dependent upon God and ask him to send us help.

⁕

### The Cost of Discipleship –

The cost of discipleship is to abandon to the One who lives for others. We have been given the life of Christ so that we will pour that life into others. From God through Jesus through us to others, as we pour ourselves into the lives of others, Jesus pours himself into us. "Give to others, and God will give to you." (Luke 6:38)

### Fallen Thinking—

- My salvation is for my sake, not for the sake of others.
- I must look out for my own needs before I can start thinking about the needs of others.

- People with needs must come to me on my own terms before I will consider helping them.
- I will only help those who deserve to be helped.

## Kingdom Thinking—
- Jesus' life flows through me when I am for others.
- I must care about the things Jesus cares about.
- I will not allow my vision of what is possible in serving others to be limited by what I see as my own strength and resources.
- Jesus calls me to serve, not be served (Mark 10:45).

## Your Choice?
Will you be a self for self or a self for others?

# 22

## BECOMING LIKE JESUS TOGETHER

*"No power in the world could have united these men for a common task, save the call of Jesus. But that call transcended all their previous divisions, and established a new and steadfast fellowship in Jesus."*

DIETRICH BONHOEFFER

*Jesus called his twelve disciples together and gave them authority to drive out evil spirits and to heal every disease and every sickness. These are the names of the twelve apostles: first, Simon (called Peter) and his brother Andrew; James and his brother John, the sons of Zebedee; Philip and Bartholomew; Thomas and Matthew, the tax collector; James son of Alphaeus, and Thaddaeus; Simon the Patriot, and Judas Iscariot, who betrayed Jesus.*

MATTHEW 10:1-4

Jesus' Objective—*To teach us that Jesus uses Christian community to bring us toward spiritual maturity.*

The disciples of Jesus have one thing in common: Jesus.

It is Jesus who calls people of all different races, nationalities, and backgrounds together to form the church, prompting you to open your home for the night to a stranger who simply comes in the name of Christ. When we answer the call of Christ, we cease to be strangers to all others who have answered his call.

It is Jesus who creates the church through the real and supernatural connection between himself and every believer. The church, then, is a group of believers, all energized by the divine nature of Christ, working together to do what the Spirit tells them.

It is Jesus who empowers us for ministry. It is only because of Jesus that we are able to love others, serving them with a supernatural sacrifice that can only be explained by the divine nature of Christ working through us.

When we follow Jesus we become citizens of the kingdom of heaven; we are subjects of the king of heaven. We live in this world; yet, we no longer look to the rules of this world for direction; instead, we look to Jesus. We no longer live as our human nature tells us to live; rather, we live as God's Spirit tells us to live (Romans 8:9).

In this sense, we are prodigals returning home, no longer subject to the laws of the far country; instead, we are now subject to the King's commands. We serve him, and we serve at his pleasure. We stay in tune with his will and we respond to the rhythms of his grace, mercy, and love.

But we are more than mere servants. Jesus declares us trustworthy friends, ready to hear what the Father is planning.

The disciples answered the call of Jesus with single-minded, obedient trust. Bonhoeffer says they left everything behind in order to follow, believing that the promises of Jesus provided greater security "than all the securities in the world."

To believe Jesus now doesn't require they take a leap of faith. They know who Jesus is; they've seen what he can do; they know he will not lie or make a false promise to them. If Jesus says they have this authority, then they can believe it is true. They hear the Word; they believe it is true, and so they are obedient to the Word's command.

The disciples lived in community with each other, but dependent upon Jesus and that meant they were consistently required to live by faith. Instead of being led by human nature, the community was led by the divine spirit and that made them sure of the things they hoped for and certain of the things they could not see (Hebrews 11:1).

We are called to live in a similar community with each other, led by the divine spirit working through each one of us as we all follow Jesus into the kingdom of heaven.

Without faith in Jesus, the church—our Christ-community—becomes nothing more than a civic club filled with people of good intentions. Such a church may be capable of remarkable service and noteworthy sacrifice, but without the Bridegroom, it can never be the bride of Christ.

A church without Jesus denies Christ's suffering, and rejection on the cross; it ignores the transformational power of his resurrection; and it cheapens the bloody price he paid to become the bridge of grace between God and man: "If Christ has not been raised from death, then we have nothing to preach and you have nothing to believe. And if Christ has not been raised, then your faith is a delusion and you are still lost in your sins" (1 Corinthians 15:14-17).

This Christless church might even celebrate Jesus, but only as a bloodless everyman who shows us how to get along, how to help others, and how to live noble lives. In the end, noble lives count for nothing. We condemn ourselves to a faithless cycle, where we rationalize our good deeds, done independent of Jesus, are good enough for God.

But Jesus will not allow us to change the rules of grace. Grace is not about doing our best. It can never be that because grace is a bloody present placed in our hands by a King who sacrificed everything and now he has the right to says our works, apart from him, will not be recognized in his kingdom: "Not everyone who calls me 'Lord, Lord' will enter the Kingdom of heaven, but only those who do what my Father in heaven wants them to do" (Matthew 7:21).

What we have in common, then, is not merely Jesus, but a belief that Jesus is who he is and that he will do what he says. We have a common faith in Jesus, believing he can be trusted and so we can be obedient. Jesus uses our obedience to increase our faith by calling us to take greater risks, but in Christian community, we find encouragement and support as we take these risks of faith.

Jesus doesn't need you perfect for the task because he's all-powerful and he can use anything and anyone for his purposes. Thinking you have to bring perfection is flawed thinking. It is pride masquerading as humility; it is a lie attempting to draw attention to yourself instead of the One who calls you.

Don't you think Jesus is extraordinarily aware of your imperfections? He knows about them from the top of his thorn-scarred head to the bottom of his nail-scarred feet.

Jesus calls; you respond with obedient trust. That is all that is required for you to serve. Bonhoeffer says any hesitancy over whether you're ready to do what Jesus tells you to do is really a form of pride that demands independence. If you doubt that, then commit to taking every decision you make today to Jesus.

See how long you last before you want Jesus to cut you slack, allowing you some independence, some "down time" from obedience to him.

Jesus calls; you obey. His call makes you ready for the task ahead. It's God's grace that you carry with you into your mission and ministry, and God's grace that energizes the good news you carry to those who need to know about God.

You have God's favor—his blessing to succeed—as you take each step toward completing the work he's given you. He's working in and around you to support your steps of faith.

He wants you—beautiful, flawed you—to show others that he's a God of redemption, a God of second chances who cares about the poor, the brokenhearted, the captives, and the prisoners. You are no different from Elijah, who "prayed earnestly that there would be no rain, and no rain fell on the land for three and a half years" (James 5:17).

God is making use of all things—pain and suffering, joy and comfort, opposition and cooperation—to reproduce and express the fullness of Christ in you. Everything that touches you is designed to de-center you from your self-for-self mentality in order to be re-centered in God's self-for-others nature.

It is Jesus who enlarges our capacity to know and express the nature of God (who is love), and he uses Christian community to do this. It is profoundly easier to live and to love 'philosophically' or in some future tense ("Someday I will . . .") than to do so in the reality of the present moment. Life together forces us out of our fantasies, where other people are always accommodating us and adjusting to all of our preferences, and then Jesus pushes us to learn to love others as he loved us, regardless of performance or appearance.

In community we learn, "The life you see me living is not 'mine,' but it is lived by faith in the Son of God, who loved me and gave himself for me." (Galatians 2:20 MSG) With the life of Christ flowing through us, we learn to love even the unlovable, and that is a unique characteristic of Christian community.

### The Cost of Discipleship –

We can no longer remain independent of others if we want to grow in Christian maturity.

### Fallen Thinking –

- My good deeds done independent of Jesus are good enough for God.
- I can mature as a Christian on my own without the help of other believers.

### Kingdom Thinking –

- Jesus calls; I obey. His call makes me ready for the task ahead.
- I must be in Christian community to mature spiritually.

### Your Choice?

Will I recognize the real and supernatural connection between myself and other believers, or will I remain independent of other believers?

# 23

## BECOMING LIKE JESUS IN OUR WORK

*"Their proclamation is clear and concise. They simply announce that the kingdom of God has drawn nigh, and summon men to repentance and faith."*
DIETRICH BONHOEFFER

*These twelve men were sent out by Jesus with the following instructions: "Do not go to any Gentile territory or any Samaritan towns. Instead, you are to go to the lost sheep of the people of Israel. Go and preach, 'The Kingdom of heaven is near!' Heal the sick, bring the dead back to life, heal those who suffer from dreaded skin diseases, and drive out demons.*

*You have received without paying, so give without being paid. Do not carry any gold, silver, or copper money in your pockets; do not carry a beggar's bag for the trip or an extra shirt or shoes or a walking stick. Workers should be given what they need.*

MATTHEW 10:5-10

Jesus' Objective—*To teach us to take care that our service for Jesus does not replace our intimacy with Jesus. Our service flows from Jesus through us to others and so our work, service, and ministry emerge from our intimacy with Jesus. "Doing things for God is the opposite of entering into what God does for you"* (Galatians 3:11a msg).

The disciples of Jesus don't get to pick and chose their work as if they're grazing through some spiritual smorgasbord. Our assignments come from Jesus, his will, his desires, his agenda. Jesus knows what is important; he knows what will be fruitful; and he knows what efforts will matter in eternity.

The disciples are free to do whatever they want, but if they want to be disciples, then they must do the work Jesus asks them to do. This means, says Bonhoeffer, they can't run off on their own impulses and inclinations. The work of the disciples is not their own; it belongs to Jesus.

We become living sacrifices, not by doing things for Jesus, but by becoming dependent on Jesus and doing the things he wants us to do. In other words, following Jesus doesn't mean we run off to do things for him; it means we stay right beside him and do the things he directs us to do. As Henry Blackaby teaches in *Experiencing God*, we look for where God is at work and we join him there. Jesus sets the agenda; Jesus sets the timetable; and Jesus empowers the work.[14]

Think about how much of the work we do in the church is independent of Jesus, and if it is independent of Jesus, it is irrelevant in the kingdom of heaven. How much of what you do is independent of Jesus and, therefore, irrelevant? Bonhoeffer notes that Jesus doesn't require we be geniuses or exceptionally creative in order to work for him. He simply requires we be obedient.

## JESUS DOESN'T EXPECT US TO DO IT ALL

Jesus lays down a limit to the disciples work. "Do not go to any Gentile territory or any Samaritan towns. Instead, you are to go to the lost sheep of the people of Israel." In this case, ignoring Jesus might have had eternal consequences because it was necessary for the gospel to be preached to the Jews first, and then, once they rejected it, the gospel could be carried to the Gentiles.

The point is we work as a grand cosmic team and God needs us to play our position. By doing what Jesus tells us to do, we are advancing the cause of the kingdom as God reclaims the fallen lives in need of redemption. He doesn't need us going off on our own, serving him at our own whim and discretion, or serving him according to our own assumptions about what we think we should be doing for him.

But it also is a signal we can't do it all and Jesus knows that. He, the Word became flesh, who dwelt among us, understands the limits of human frailty, exhaustion and stress. When we do what Jesus tells us to do it eliminates so much of the busy work in our lives. It frees us from the tyranny of thinking we have to do everything so that we are free to do what we are called to do. We are simply responsible for the things he assigns us and we don't need to feel guilty that we can't do it all.

Hear this: This doesn't mean, *We can only do what we can do*, in the sense that we give a bit of ourselves to Jesus while we fill our lives with things we want to do. Rather, it means, *We can only do what Jesus tells us to do*.

This also means, as Bonhoeffer notes, that we cannot do the work of God *without authorization*. If we do work for Jesus that he never asked us to do, it will be empty of the promises he provides for provision and success. We can do work for Jesus and still be faithless.

When we do the work (ministry, service, evangelism) on our own terms, then it requires no faith and so we are working without faith. *We are working faithlessly*; we may even accomplish a great deal but it isn't recognizable in the kingdom of heaven. We are not doing what Jesus wants us to do and that means we are in disobedience to him.

Jesus always has his eye on the end-game. He sees the final judgment and his perspective keeps him riveted to his mission. In the sense of a coach, Jesus sees the big picture and he is training us to play our position because there is a whole team at work. We're to stay at our position, the one that God created us to fill in the body of Christ.

The bottom line is this: Our ministry is defined by Jesus. We do not minister for Jesus if we set the terms. In the same way, our discipleship is defined by Jesus. We cannot call ourselves disciples of Jesus if we set the terms of our discipleship.

## THE KINGDOM OF HEAVEN IS NEAR!

The disciples proclaim the coming of the kingdom of heaven. They have learned from Jesus this is not a future event but that Jesus creates an immediate and singular bridge into the kingdom.

Jesus is the narrow gate we must go through to enter the kingdom: *"I am telling you the truth: I am the gate for the sheep. All others who came before me are thieves and robbers, but the sheep did not listen to them. I am the gate. Those who come in by me will be saved; they will come in and go out and find pasture. The thief comes only in order to steal, kill, and destroy. I have come in order that you might have life—life in all its fullness"* (John 10:7-10).

The disciples are becoming reflections of Jesus just as we are to become reflections of Jesus. By following him in obedience, the disciples have learned to think and act like Jesus. They are becoming confident of their new citizenship in the kingdom of heaven; that is, they are becoming Christlike.

*"I have made you known to those you gave me out of the world,"* says Jesus. *"They belonged to you, and you gave them to me. They have obeyed your word, and now they know that everything you gave me comes from you. I gave them the message that you gave me, and they received it; they know that it is true that I came from you, and they believe that you sent me"* (John 17:6-8).

When the disciples show up, it is as if Jesus is showing up—and to prove his presence *in this case*—Jesus authorizes them to heal the sick, bring the dead back to life, cleanse lepers, and drive out demons. *Just like Jesus.*

## JUST LIKE JESUS DOES (JLJD!)

In this way, Bonhoeffer says, "The message becomes an event, and the event confirms the message. The kingdom of God, Jesus Christ, the forgiveness of sins, the justification of the sinner through faith, all this is identical with the destruction of the devil's power, the healing of the sick and raising of the dead."

The proclamation of the gospel is the word of the Almighty God, Bonhoeffer notes, and it is an event, a miracle. The path is clear; *the bridge is built*; the narrow gate is open for those willing to follow Jesus and accept the cost of his grace.

The disciples are unified by their Christlikeness, which foreshadows the unity of all those who believe. "It is the one Christ who passes through the land in the person of his twelve messengers and performs his work," says Bonhoeffer. "The sovereign grace with which they are equipped is the creative and redemptive Word of God."

Just as our prayers call the kingdom down to earth, the proclamation of the gospel is an aggressive act meant to free the captives from this fallen world. It takes back the ground—and the lives—that the enemy holds captive. The light pushes the darkness away (John 1:4-5).

## DISCIPLES CANNOT BE SPIRITUAL PACIFISTS

*Jesus, again, allows no middle ground.* When we follow Jesus, we join his battle with the enemy. The apostle John says the message we have heard from the Son is this: "God is light, and there is no darkness at all in him. If, then, we say that we have fellowship with him, yet at the same time live in the darkness, we are lying both in our words and in our actions. But if we live in the light—just as he is in the light—then we have fellowship with one another, and the blood of Jesus, his Son, purifies us from every sin" (1 John 1:5-7).

The cost of discipleship includes our break with the foolish notion that we can follow Jesus and remain spiritual pacifists. "This is no afternoon athletic contest that we'll walk away from and forget about in a couple of hours," says the apostle Paul. "This is for keeps, a life-or-death fight to the finish against the Devil and all his angels" (Ephesians 6:11-12 MSG).

This is an important point because, as long as the enemy keeps us lulled into believing we are non-combatants in the war for souls, we will be lackadaisical and wimpy in our approach to evangelism, discipleship and spiritual warfare. What's more, we will continue to believe in the mythological world we call real, where we assume there is no connection between the things we do and the spiritual world.

## "FREELY YOU HAVE RECEIVED, FREELY GIVE"

We are chosen for ministry by Jesus and equipped for ministry by Jesus. It has nothing to do with what we bring to the table and so, Bonhoeffer says, we are stealing from Jesus when we expect, or demand, special rights or privileges because we serve God.

The gifts the disciples have been given are not "personal possessions which they could trade for other goods," says Bonhoeffer. What we have been given freely, we should freely give. This is, in truth, the cycle of the kingdom of heaven. Jesus gives to us; we give to others; and so Jesus gives to us again. It is a cycle of love and trust and looking out for others instead of ourselves, serving others without expecting anything in return.

This does not mean that those in full-time vocational ministry cannot be paid. Jesus says they should be given what they need, the *workman approved* as described by the apostle Paul (2 Timothy 2:14).

Bonhoeffer asks, "And if this battle with the powers of Satan for the souls of men, this renunciation of all personal dignity, and of the goods and joy of the world for the sake of the poor and miserable and ill-used, is not work, what is?"

At issue is our motive for ministry. We're to serve in such a way, says Bonhoeffer, that others will see we have "plenty of riches to give away, but desire nothing for [ourselves], neither possessions, nor admiration nor regard, and least of all their gratitude."

Jesus calls us to make a ruthless assessment of why we serve him? Why do we serve others? What draws us to ministry? Is it out of loving obedience to him? Is it because we believe and we act upon our belief? Or are we motivated by praise from others? Do we serve because it makes us feel good about ourselves or maintains an image of what we think a nice person would be like? Do we serve out of guilt? Do we serve for prestige, or power, or money?

The motivation of our ministry is revealed by our ruffled feelings when no one appreciates what we do. As Rick Warren notes in his book, *The Purpose Driven Life*, one way to determine if you have the heart of a servant is to see how you respond when someone treats you like a servant.

Jesus limits what the disciples should take with them to the barest of necessities. Bonhoeffer compares it to just enough to make it through a day if we know we'll be spending the night at a friend's house. He says when we show up with enough to meet our needs but not so little that we appear as beggars looking for a hand-out, we show others we are not looking to profit off of them as we minister to them.

The point is: We trust God to provide for us and not those we serve. Bonhoeffer says, "This shall be an expression of their faith, not in men, but in their heavenly Father who sent them and will care for them. It is this that will make their Gospel credible, for they proclaim the coming Kingdom of God."

We are to be totally and wholly dependent upon God to fulfill his promises. Jesus calls us to a sacrificial service, where we do what he tells us to do regardless of how much it will be noticed or appreciated.

*When you come to a town or village, go in and look for someone who is willing to welcome you, and stay with him until you leave that place. When you go into a house, say, 'Peace be with you.' If the people in that house welcome you, let your greeting of peace remain; but if they do not welcome you, then take back your greeting. And if some home or town will not welcome you or listen to you, then leave that place and shake the dust off your feet. I assure you that on the Judgment Day God will show more mercy to the people of Sodom and Gomorrah than to the people of that town!* (Matthew 10:11-15)

Bonhoeffer notes, as the disciples enter a house during their journey, they're told to use the same word of greeting as Jesus, their master: "Peace be with this house" (Luke 10:5). "This is no empty formula, for it immediately brings the power of the peace of God on those who 'are worthy of it,'" says Bonhoeffer.

We come representing Jesus. As the apostle Paul says, "We're speaking for Christ himself now: Become friends with God; he's already a friend with you" (2 Corinthians 5:20 MSG). We bring the good news that Jesus has entered our conflict with God, bringing a ruthless love that will not stop until we have surrendered to God.

We bring the good news that our savior and mediator is benevolent in victory, able to say, "Go in peace and be freed from your suffering" (Mark 5:34 NIV). We represent a peace that "transcends all understanding," yet, a peace founded in our belief that Jesus will fulfill his promises. It is a peace forged in forgiveness and formed by the Father's heart (Luke 1:79 NIV; Philippians 4:7 NIV; see also Proverbs 3:5–6).

And there will be those who will not listen and they will reject us, but in rejecting us, they are actually rejecting Jesus. This is a sign of kingdom thinking growing strong within us—that we can see past the rejection of others into the reality of eternity. It is not our job—not our work—to plead and beg them into the kingdom. We do not have to make them listen to us or insist they believe the truth.

We are no longer responsible for them, says Jesus, underscoring that he will authorize our efforts and expand or limit our ministry according to his needs, his will, his plan. We are told to stop our own efforts and hand them over to God. We're to shake the dust from our feet and leave them to God's judgment.

Rejection is a risk Jesus is willing to take on his mission for you and he calls us to face rejection in our service to him. When we face rejection, Jesus is not disappointed in us; rather, his grief is with those who refuse to listen: "If you, even you, had only known on this day what would bring you peace—but now it is hidden from your eyes" (Luke 19:42 NIV).

### The Cost of Discipleship—

Life flows from God through Jesus to us. The cost of discipleship is that we stop allowing our worries and anxieties to dictate the work we do; instead, we rest in the peace of God flowing through us. We stop doing for God and start recognizing what he is doing in us—and we join the work of Jesus, serving others from his life that flows from us to others.

### Fallen Thinking—

- I must figure out what I think needs to be done and then do it.
- Ministry is ego-driven—"It all depends on me".
- I have veto power over the commands of Jesus.
- I'm not always sure he knows what he is doing and so I want to understand his plan before I decide what to do.
- God's plan revolves around my ministry and so my ministry is more important than others.

### Kingdom Thinking—

- Jesus calls me to specific ministry *in his name*.
- My ministry emerges from the life of Christ within me, not from external pressures or circumstances.
- By being obedient to Jesus, I find the work God created me to do; that is, I find my purpose in life through my obedience to the commands of Jesus.
- My assignment is part of God's overall plan to bring others into the kingdom of heaven.
- Working independent of Jesus, even with the best of intentions, means I am working against God's plan and that means I am in rebellion to God.

### Your Choice?

Will you join Jesus in his work or will you demand he come over and join your own, independent efforts?

# 24

## BECOMING LIKE JESUS
## THROUGH PERSECUTION

*"Nothing can happen to them without Jesus knowing of it."*
DIETRICH BONHOEFFER

*Listen! I am sending you out just like sheep to a pack of wolves. You must
be as cautious as snakes and as gentle as doves. Watch out, for there will be
those who will arrest you and take you to court, and they will whip you in the
synagogues. For my sake you will be brought to trial before rulers and kings, to
tell the Good News to them and to the Gentiles.*

*When they bring you to trial, do not worry about what you are going to say
or how you will say it; when the time comes, you will be given what you will
say. For the words you will speak will not be yours; they will come from the
Spirit of your Father speaking through you.*

*People will hand over their own brothers to be put to death, and fathers
will do the same to their children; children will turn against their parents and
have them put to death. Everyone will hate you because of me. But whoever
holds out to the end will be saved. When they persecute you in one town, run
away to another one. I assure you that you will not finish your work in all the
towns of Israel before the Son of Man comes.*

*No pupil is greater than his teacher; no slave is greater than his master.
So a pupil should be satisfied to become like his teacher, and a slave like
his master. If the head of the family is called Beelzebul, the members of the
family will be called even worse names!*

MATTHEW 10:16-25

Jesus' Objective—*To teach us to see persecution as confirmation
that the righteousness of Christ is flowing through us.*

Jesus taught that his yoke is easy (Matthew 11:30) but he never said our lives would become easier when we followed him. The truth is, our lives will likely become harder because we're forced to face the harsh reality of life without delusions. We can't keep pretending everything is okay. We've seen the destructive nature of sin; we understand its real costs; we know we can't wash it all away, only the blood of Jesus can do that.

Where we once could lie or steal or cheat to get what we wanted, now we're in supernatural union with Jesus and we're required to deal with the reality of our circumstances and relationships, using weapons of Jesus, such as honesty, humility, grace, love, prayer, obedience, and by allowing the Holy Spirit to guide us.

Where we once could escape the heartaches of the present through pornographic fantasy, drugs, alcohol, or evil little rationalizations meant to force reality into our own convenient view, now we're expected to stay in the present—to be all there—and face our difficulties head-on by submitting them to the truth, the Word of God, Jesus, our Brother and King.

To suggest the Christian life is a gateway to problem-free, stress-less living is a sign of fallen thinking. Our lives in Christ are meant to be extraordinary, incredible, meaningful, and purposeful but never trouble-free. We're to step into the will of God and stay there, trusting he has our best interests at heart, even though he tells us that circumstances seem so bad that we doubt his promises (Jeremiah 29:11, Romans 8:28, Philippians 4:13).

Rather than taking us out of the problems of life, making us appear amazing to others, he keeps us in the pressure-cooker so others can see how a life connected to Jesus confronts problems in a very different way than a life disconnected from the divine nature. We handle difficult situations differently because we are energized by the Holy Spirit; we respond to hardship like people from the kingdom of heaven, not like people in rebellion to God or unaware of God or unrepentant before God.

When we act as if God is not involved in our circumstances, we deny his power in our lives. We go to church, we meet in our small groups, we quote the Bible, but when the rubber hits the road, we know it isn't true and so we handle things according to our human nature. We respond with defensiveness, blame, shame, anger, hatred, pride, fear, and self-centeredness.

Anybody can do that. *Anybody not connected to Jesus*. We are, in that moment, no different from those who appear to have faith but reject its real power (2 Timothy 3:5).

Part of what Jesus is trying to get the disciples to see is that our response in situations of stress and danger is based upon our trust in him. Is God involved in your circumstances or not? When we respond from our human nature, instead of submitting to the divine nature working within us, we expose a deep, inner distrust of Jesus. Our actions show we believe him incapable of understanding the stress and danger of life.

But when we respond from the truth that we are connected to Jesus, we prove that we believe "he that is within us is greater than he who is in the world" (1 John 4:4). We may be hard pressed on every side, but God keeps us from being crushed; perplexed, but God lifts us from the pits of despair; persecuted, but God stands by our side; struck down, but indestructible because we're filled with the incorruptible Spirit of God (2 Corinthians 4).

The call of Christ requires us to rely upon him when we come up against the difficulties of life, particularly when we come up against the enemies of Jesus who seek to persecute us. Because Christ dwells in us, we know we do not face these trials alone; any attack on us is an attack on Jesus. Our identity is so wrapped within Jesus that our enemies cannot separate us from him.

Jesus says we're to be as cunning as snakes and as harmless as doves. Recognizing the difference between the two isn't always easy. How can we tell whether we are being wise spiritually or just crafty in a worldly way? Bonhoeffer asks, "Who is there to let us know when we are running away from suffering through cowardice, or running after it through temerity?"

We're not really able to judge that for ourselves. Often, we don't even understand our own motives. We may claim to know what drives us, but we have the unique human ability to deceive ourselves (1 John 1:8).

The answer is clear, that Christ takes us to the hidden frontier of the kingdom of heaven, where we learn from him what to say and what to do. So we need "not worry about what you are going to say or how you will say it" because we will be given what to say. "For the words you will speak will not be yours; they will come from the Spirit of your Father speaking through you," says Jesus.

But we must obediently believe the Spirit of God is working within us, giving us the right words to say and teaching us to think and act like Jesus. Bonhoeffer says, "Jesus never called his disciples into a state of uncertainty, but to one of supreme certainty. That is why his warning can only summon them to abide by the Word. Where the Word is, there shall the disciple be."

We abide in the Word when we obediently believe God goes before and comes behind us in all our circumstances (Psalm 139:5). We are like sheep among wolves, Bonhoeffer notes: "defenseless, powerless, sore pressed and beset with great danger." But nothing happens to any of us without the Lord knowing all about it. In fact, Jesus says God actively engineers circumstances so we can tell others the good news. The Word teaches us what is true: "It corrects us when we are wrong and teaches us to do what is right. God uses it to prepare and equip [us] to do every good work" (2 Timothy 3:16b-17 NLT).

In other words, we must allow God to interpret the situations we face. Only he is capable of understanding all the facts and only he sees the significance of every detail.

The New Testament provides an illustration of this. When Paul was on his way to Jerusalem, a prophet named Agabus came to see him. He took Paul's belt and he tied it around his own hands and feet, telling the apostle, "The Holy Spirit says, 'In this way the Jews of Jerusalem will bind the owner of this belt and will hand him over to the Gentiles'" (Acts 21:11 NIV). Hearing this, Paul's friends immediately tried to talk him out of going to Jerusalem, but he went anyway, saying, "I am ready not only to be bound, but also to die in Jerusalem for the name of the Lord Jesus" (Acts 21:13 NIV).

What the Holy Spirit told Agabus was fact; Paul was bound and handed over to the Gentiles in Jerusalem. But this is an illustration of why we should always let God interpret the facts. He has a heavenly point-of-view, able to see the whole truth and nothing but the truth.

The facts, by themselves, may not reveal the whole truth.

The greater truth was that Paul's arrest became the means for getting him to Rome, which he'd been longing to visit for some time. Once in Rome, Paul was placed under house arrest, forcing him to stay in one place after so many years on the road as a missionary. Bound in chains, Paul began to write letters to the congregations he'd helped plant, and some of those letters are available to us as books in the New Testament.

It was a fact, then, that Paul would be arrested in Jerusalem, but God had a different interpretation of what the facts meant. He planned to use the arrest to further Paul's ministry, not only in Paul's generation, but all the way into our own.

We may gather facts, but we must leave it up to God to interpret them.

Jesus continues to teach us to look to the end-game. We are engaged in a spiritual battle that is "no afternoon athletic contest that we'll walk away from and forget about in a couple of hours. This is for keeps, a life-or-death fight to the finish . . ." (Ephesians 6:12 MSG).

The people before us are not our enemy; rather, they, like we once were, are lost in the enemy's dark kingdom and we offer the light they need to find their way to Jesus. We know the return of Jesus is imminent and Bonhoeffer says "that fact is more certain than that we shall be able to finish our work in his service, more certain than our own death." He says, "Only be will he blessed who remains loyal to Jesus and his word until the end."

The more we become like Jesus, the more we will suffer and be persecuted. Jesus says, "No pupil is greater than his teacher; no slave is greater than his master. So a pupil should be satisfied to become like his teacher, and a slave like his master" (Matthew 10:24-25a).

But as we are persecuted, we can find comfort in that it affirms we are on the right path, following Jesus on the narrow way into the kingdom of heaven. Our courage and confidence is *in Christ* and his truth, the reality of "Christ in you, the hope of glory" (Colossians 1:27 NIV).

If you obediently believed this to be true, how will you respond to the trials and tribulations of life? Or, looked at from the other side, what does your response to the trials and tribulations of life reveal about what you truly believe? What does your behavior indicate regarding your trust in Jesus?

### The Cost of Discipleship –
As the righteousness of Jesus flows through you, you will be persecuted. This is part of the cost of your union with Christ.

### Fallen Thinking—
- I am being persecuted; God, why are you letting this happen to me?
- What God is telling me doesn't make sense; I have the facts; I need to make a decision.

### Kingdom Thinking—
- I am being persecuted; God, this hurts, but I know you have my best interests in mind, I know you have a loving nature, and I know this is the result of the life of Christ flowing through me. This is the cost of grace, but I also know this shows I will share in Christ's inheritance.
- God, this doesn't make sense to me, but I will let you interpret the circumstances. You have a better perspective than me and there may be something I am not seeing. Isn't that what faith must be? Trusting God, even if we don't agree.

### Your Choice?
We're to step into the will of God and stay there, trusting he has our best interests at heart, even though he tells us that circumstances seem so bad that we doubt his promises (Jeremiah 29:11, Romans 8:28, Philippians 4:13).

# 25

## BECOMING LIKE JESUS IN OUR FAITH

*"The same God who sees no sparrow fall to the ground without his knowledge and will, allows nothing to happen, except it be good and profitable for his children and the cause for which they stand. We are in God's hands. Therefore, 'Fear not.'"*

DIETRICH BONHOEFFER

*So do not be afraid of people. Whatever is now covered up will be uncovered, and every secret will be made known. What I am telling you in the dark you must repeat in broad daylight, and what you have heard in private you must announce from the housetops. Do not be afraid of those who kill the body but cannot kill the soul; rather be afraid of God, who can destroy both body and soul in hell. For only a penny you can buy two sparrows, yet not one sparrow falls to the ground without your Father's consent. As for you, even the hairs of your head have all been counted. So do not be afraid; you are worth much more than many sparrows!*

MATTHEW 10:26-39

Jesus' Objective—*To teach us that our fears are an opportunity to develop an intimate trust in Jesus.*

The emotion of fear is not a sign of unbelief, but to allow fear to shape and condition what you do is a sign of unbelief. In other words, feeling fear doesn't always mean you are not trusting God. It is a God-given emotion meant to alert you to potential danger. The problem is when you allow fear to set the agenda so that your decisions are being made out of fear instead of faith.

There are two reasons why the disciples of Jesus need not fear.

**First, we abide with Christ**; that is, we are in union with Jesus and our connection to him, and to God through him, draws us into the protective bubble wrap of God's grace. We are embedded in the righteousness of Jesus and "neither death nor life, neither angels nor demons, neither the present nor the future, nor any powers, neither height nor depth, nor anything else in all creation, will be able to separate us from the love of God that is in Christ Jesus our Lord" (Romans 8:37-39 NIV).

Jesus says no one can snatch us away from him and no one can snatch us away from the Father's care (John 10:28-30). What's more, God knows us; he loves us, and he accepts us (1 Corinthians 13:12, Psalm 119, Ephesians 1:6).

We are known, loved, accepted, and protected by God. Jesus says "I give them real and eternal life. They are protected from the Destroyer for good. No one can steal them from out of my hand. The Father who put them under my care is so much greater than the Destroyer and Thief. No one could ever get them away from him" (John 10:28-29 MSG; see also, 1 Corinthians 13:12, Psalm 119, Ephesians 1:6).

Secured safely in Christ's costly grace, God's love sweeps away our fear because, the apostle John says, fear has to do with punishment and there's no need for us to fear punishment since, covered by the righteousness of Jesus, we are no longer under God's judgment (1 John 4:18).

Since we no longer fear God, who else or what else is there for us to fear? "If God is for us, who can be against us? Certainly not God, who did not even keep back his own Son, but offered him for us all! He gave us his Son—will he not also freely give us all things" (Romans 8:31-32).

**Second, our future is certain.** The disciples of Jesus have no reason to fear the future. We won't grow weary and lose heart if we "fix our eyes on Jesus, the author and perfecter of our faith, who for the joy set before him endured the cross, scorning its shame, and sat down at the right hand of the throne of God" (Hebrews 12:1-3 NIV).

Jesus is taking us down the narrow path through the narrow gate into the kingdom of heaven and all we have to do is follow him in single-minded obedience.

No looking to the left or looking to the right; if we stay focused on him, we have no need to fear.

Fear is based on the false belief that terrible things will happen if we make a mistake. It is a fear that God is not big enough to handle the things in life that are bigger than us.

But your fears reveal your faith, or lack of it.

Your focus will determine your behavior *and* it will influence your faith.

## DO YOU TRUST FEAR MORE THAN GOD?

When the Israelites first approached the borders of Canaan, Moses sent scouts into the promised land to assess the situation. Ten of the scouts came back with reports that focused on the giants in the land, men so big and powerful the scouts feared they could not be defeated.

However, two of the scouts focused on the promise from God that he would hand the land over to the Israelites. One of those scouts, Caleb, silenced the others when he said, "We should go up and take possession of the land, for we can certainly do it" (Numbers 13:30 NIV). Caleb trusted God instead of trusting his own fear. The opposite of fear is faith, the belief that Jesus is capable of handling anything we may face in life. But operating out of faith means we must rely on Jesus, remaining *dependent* on him to see us through any issue.

Once again, Jesus brings us to a choice: Will we trust God or will we trust our own fears?

The Bible says, "The fear of the LORD is the beginning of wisdom" (Proverbs 9:10a NIV). In other words, we hold God in reverence, recognizing his sovereignty, authority, and omnipotence—his ability to protect us in any situation. And we reach that level of intimate trust by knowing the Father and understanding his character. "If you know the Holy One, you have understanding" (Proverbs 9:10b).

We know and understand the Father by following Jesus. "To see me is to see the Father," says Jesus. ". . . Don't you believe that I am in the Father and the Father is in me? The words that I speak to you aren't mere words. I don't just make them up on my own. The Father who resides in me crafts each word into a divine act" (John 14:9b-10 MSG).

As Jesus teaches us kingdom thinking, we learn to see our fear as a way to deepen our trust in Jesus. Rather than running from what we fear, we can run to where we place our faith—to the person we most trust—Jesus, our advocate and mediator before God. We already know that Jesus will do anything necessary to protect us, even if it means dying on the cross for us.

Of course, our fear may have to do with sin. When we walk in disobedience to Jesus—when we are not abiding with him, particularly because of our pursuit of sin—we open the door for the devil to push fearful thoughts toward us. The thing to do is to take those fears to Jesus and allow him to show us our sin. We can then confess our sin and begin abiding in Jesus again.

## SO DO NOT BE AFRAID OF PEOPLE

"Men can do them no harm, for the power of men ceases with the death of the body," says Bonhoeffer. "But they must overcome the fear of death with the fear of God."

When we fear what other people may think, say, or do, we let them steal the freedom we have in Jesus. In a sense, they put us back under the law and under the fear of judgment—and that means we live in the mythology that they have a greater power over our lives than God, the Creator and Master of the universe.

Instead, we need to get our thinking right. God is bigger than anyone or any-thing. God is in control at all times. Instead of fearing men, who at best can kill us, we should, instead, fear God who has the authority to decide where we will spend eternity. Stop seeing simply the shadows that are right in front of you and start seeing things from the reality of life in the kingdom of heaven.

Bonhoeffer notes this is a black and white decision: "Those who are still afraid of men have no fear of God, and those who have fear of God have ceased to be afraid of men. All preachers of the gospel will do well to recollect this saying daily."

## FAITH SHOULD SET THE AGENDA

The struggle is that we, both passively and aggressively, insist fear set the agenda. But fear pushes us into a life based on self-interest. We make choices based on our fears and not on our faith in Jesus. In fear, we look out for ourselves and that means *we act exactly like those who have no faith.*

We must face the question, "Do I trust Jesus to keep his promises or not?" (Would your life change if the answer was "Yes.")

When we stop thinking like fallen people, we realize that our fear and lack of faith is not really about God; it is about our inability to trust and to let go of our need to understand everything we face. In a sense, we demand our right to fear something or someone unless we have a full understanding of what is going on and that makes a god out of our understanding. That is idolatry because it lifts our need to understand above the one, true God.

Our fears, then, terrorize us into chronic spiritual immaturity where we're held hostage to our worries and doubts. It keeps us from developing an intimate trust in Jesus and keeps us isolated. Fear whispers in our ear that we face danger alone, that God is unaware of our plight and that Jesus is unavailable in our time of need.

Worse, when fear suggests we are alone, it implies the Holy Spirit is no longer active in our lives. And that is nothing short of heresy; yet we act on this false belief every time we give our fears greater reverence than God (1 John 4:4). And when we think we face our fears alone, it diminishes our fellowship with other believers because we're afraid to embrace the kind of authentic and transparent relationships common to the kingdom of heaven.

## FAITH SHOULD SHAPE OUR LIVES

Jesus says fear should no longer shape our lives. It keeps us out-of-step with him, and he will stop at nothing, including a bloody cross, to eliminate fear from our lives. He commands that we begin making decisions in faith and not in fear.

Bonhoeffer notes the things we fear come and go but God is always there and always faithful. And God is not surprised by the evil men do. He is not surprised by who leads in government. Even when we face systemic evil, such as the Nazi regime Bonhoeffer opposed, we can trust that God is aware of our circumstances.

Is it possible God was not aware of that the Roman Empire employed cruci-fixion? Of course God knew; nevertheless, he sent his Only Son into the mess. He used devilish circumstances and flawed men to bring about his own will and purposes. Bonhoeffer says, "If we fall into the hands of men, and meet suffering and death from their violence, we are none the less certain that everything comes from God."

In Jesus, we find an uncommon safety that promises God is present even when we face our greatest fears. The choice is, will we believe God when he says, "I alone know the plans I have for you, plans to bring you prosperity and not disaster, plans to bring about the future you hope for" (Jeremiah 29:11). Within this promise is an acknowledgement from God that we may, for a time, view his plans as disastrous, perhaps even evil; yet we are still told, 'Fear not!'

If God knows when a sparrow falls and you are worth more than the sparrow, don't you think the Father will take care of you? Jesus is teaching us kingdom thinking. This is the way our minds were created to think before the devil whispered doubt and distrust into the neural network of our brains. Jesus, again, pushes us to a choice: will we trust our fears or will we trust the Word of God?

The point is we are in God's hands and *so what we fear can never be viewed separate from that truth*. Fear not; God is taking care of you. Jesus is not suggesting we will no longer face terrible situations once we stop being afraid. Jesus is not naive about the reality of evil in this world; the men who crucified Jesus were an incarnation of that evil; yet, God used that for his own great purposes.

All things—*even the things we fear*—work together for the good of those who love God and are called by Jesus to his purposes. Think of the worst thing anyone can do to you and understand, in faith, that God can redeem that evil in some way.

How would your perspective change if you trusted that God is taking all the bad things in your life and re-creating them to bring good into your life?

God, and our Savior, Jesus, keep a constant eye on the end-game, the final judgment. Jesus says there will come a time when he will wipe away our tears; he will vindicate us; we will see justice roll down like a mighty river flowing from the kingdom of heaven. What is hidden will be exposed; what appears good will be shown for the evil that it is; what appears foolish will be shown to be God's wisdom.

There will be a day of judgment, but it will not be based on who did best and who did worst; instead, it will be based on who stands under the law and who stands under grace.

And, in the end, there is the hopeful possibility that we will see God's redemptive power transform the hearts of our enemies, eliminating all fear through the power of divine love. We're to "keep our eyes fixed on Jesus, on whom our faith depends from beginning to end," fearing God instead of men, for in our struggle against sin and evil we "have not yet had to resist to the point of being killed" (Hebrews 12:2, 4).

And we need not fear death because, unlike Moses, who approached God in fear and trembling, we now *come to the joyful gathering of God's first-born, whose names are written in heaven. [We] come to God, who is the judge of all people, and to the spirits of good people made perfect. [We] come to Jesus, who arranged the new covenant, and to the sprinkled blood that promises much better things than does the blood of Abel"* (Hebrews 12:23-24).

Because of our union with Jesus we will "receive a kingdom that cannot be shaken. Let us be grateful and worship God in a way that will please him, with reverence and awe; because our God is indeed a destroying fire" (Hebrews 12:24). What God burns away in our lives is isolated only to the things we do not need, or that will hinder us, on our journey to the kingdom of heaven.

*Those who declare publicly that they belong to me, I will do the same for them before my Father in heaven. But those who reject me publicly, I will reject before my Father in heaven.*

*Do not think that I have come to bring peace to the world. No, I did not come to bring peace, but a sword. I came to set sons against their fathers, daughters against their mothers, daughters-in-law against their mothers-in-law; your worst enemies will be the members of your own family. Those who love their father or mother more than me are not fit to be my disciples; those who love their son or daughter more than me are not fit to be my disciples. Those who do not take up their cross and follow in my steps are not fit to be my disciples.*

*Those who try to gain their own life will lose it; but those who lose their life for my sake will gain it.* Matthew 10:32-39

Will we be loyal to our fears or loyal to Jesus?

Jesus says we should know this: if we fear we will lose out on life by following him, the truth is we will lose it all anyway, and at the same time, we will lose out on the real life we're searching for.

On the other hand, if we abandon our fears and follow him, he will lead us into the kingdom of heaven, where we will find the life we always hoped for.

It is a very practical decision unless you're trapped in the kind of fallen thinking that tells us disposable things and temporary relationships are the end all and be all of the universe. When someone argues that following Jesus is impractical, it shows they do not have a clue about the kingdom of heaven. "The Message that points to Christ on the Cross seems like sheer silliness to those hellbent on destruction, but for those on the way of salvation it makes perfect sense," says the apostle Paul (1 Corinthians 1:18 MSG).

When *we* suggest the commands of Jesus are impractical or unrealistic, we show we're still not thinking like citizens of the kingdom of heaven. His commands may appear impractical or unrealistic, but, with obedient trust, we will know they are the perfect steps to take in the kingdom of heaven.

And so Jesus comes with his eye on the final judgment. "The time is short. Eternity is long. It is the time of decision," says Bonhoeffer. "If we have been true to Jesus in this life, he will be true to us in eternity. But if we have been ashamed of our Lord and of his name, he will likewise be ashamed of us and deny us. The final decision must be made while we are still on earth."

With his cross, Jesus brings peace, notes Bonhoeffer. "But the cross is the sword God wields on earth." The Word of God is "sharp as a surgeon's scalpel, cutting through everything, whether doubt or defense, laying us open to listen and obey." (Hebrews 4:12 MSG) Again, Jesus slices across our loyalties, demanding that we chose him as the priority. The Word of God slices through our motives, separating anything that is not of God from those things that are of God.

Everything must be brought to the feet of Jesus. The life of Christ flows from him through us to others and so everything must be subjugated to the reality of Jesus in our lives. Again, Jesus stresses how pervasive his presence should be in our lives: "Those who love their father or mother more than me are not fit to be my disciples; those who love their son or daughter more than me are not fit to be my disciples."

Jesus will not share his prominence in your life with anyone else. He also says no disciple is exempt from carrying the cross he or she is assigned. This means, for instance, we cannot use our children as an excuse to disobey the commands of Jesus. If Jesus says move to this neighborhood, we cannot say, "But Jesus, that's not where I want to raise my kids. I'll move there after they have grown." The thing is, most of us do not even ask Jesus where we should live. We just decide based on human wisdom and financial circumstances.

Jesus is not an important part of your life; he is your life. His life envelops and saturates all that you are. If you try to find your life apart from Jesus, you will lose it; but if you lose your life in Christ, then you will live an extraordinary life energized by the life of Christ within you.

❧

### The Cost of Discipleship—
You are in union with Jesus; his life flows from him to you. He is there with you, even when you fear. When you are afraid, you must come to Jesus in obedient trust (Psalms 56:3)

### Fallen Thinking—
- I fear what others may do, think, or say about me.
- My faith has nothing to do with my fears.
- I will make my decisions based on what I fear.
- I fear what others may do, think, or say about me.

### Kingdom Thinking—
- There is no need for me to be afraid because God is in control of this situation.
- 'God, why am I afraid? What is causing my fear?'
- Jesus says I should not fear and that means I have a choice. I can choose to respond in faith instead of fear. "When I am afraid, I will trust in you. In God, whose word I praise, in God I trust; I will not be afraid. What can mortal man do to me?" (Psalms 56:3-4 NIV) "The fear of human opinion disables; trusting in God protects you from that" (Proverbs 29:25 MSG).

### Your Choice?

When I am afraid, will I trust in Jesus or trust in my fears? Your fear can help reveal the places where you aren't yet trusting in Jesus. Don't stay stuck in your fear. Jesus wants to move you past that into a place with your fears are replaced by faith. Follow him and learn to obediently trust.

# 26

## BECOMING LIKE JESUS TO OTHERS

*"When they are welcomed into a house, Christ enters with them. They are bearers of his presence. They bring with them the most precious gift in the world, the gift of Jesus Christ. And with him they bring God the Father, and that means indeed forgiveness and salvation, life and bliss. That is the reward and fruit of their toil and suffering."*

DIETRICH BONHOEFFER

*Whoever welcomes you welcomes me; and whoever welcomes me welcomes the one who sent me. Whoever welcomes God's messenger because he is God's messenger, will share in his reward. And whoever welcomes a good man because he is good, will share in his reward. You can be sure that whoever gives even a drink of cold water to one of the least of these my followers because he is my follower, will certainly receive a reward.*

MATTHEW 10:40-42

Jesus' Objective—*To teach us that we are connected to other believers through our connection to Jesus.*

Your role in life has changed. Your long-term assignment is no longer looking out for your own interests. You now represent the interests of Jesus. You're the face of Jesus, showing up in the lives of others on his behalf. You show up in the hospital; you show up at the funeral; you show up at the wedding; you show up across the fence as you talk to your neighbors.

Your ambassadorship is more than a mere job; you are "speaking for Christ, as though God himself were making his appeal" through you, pleading "on Christ's behalf: let God change you from enemies into his friends!" (2 Corinthians 5:20).

In order to be a faithful ambassador, we have to come in person. Jesus came in person, not as a religion, a set of laws, or as a tract left at the door. He brings us into the personal embrace of a passionate and loving union with the divine nature and you come proclaiming that we can "seek after God, and not just grope around in the dark but actually *find* him . . . . He's not remote; he's *near*" (Acts 17:27 MSG).

We live in a world where the absence of personal touch is glaring and where there is a belief that the impersonal is able to save us, such as through better organization, purer methodology, and more pervasive technology. We expect all this from the world, but we shouldn't tolerate it in the body of Christ, where we supernaturally connected to the Creator and Protector of all that is personal (1 John 4:6 MSG).

## BOUND TO ONE ANOTHER

Since we're called to be like Jesus, we must personally interact and invest in one another's lives and to do it in a way that is meaningful. Jesus commands us to bind ourselves to each other, caring for one another the way Jesus cares for us. When the world asks to see who the Word of God is and how he personally loves us, we can say, "Watch how we love one another."

Jesus gave the world the right to judge the authenticity of our faith by how much we love one another. We prove our faith in Christ, not by the rules we keep, but by the love we give. Our love for one another is a tangible and contagious reflection of God's love—allowing the world to witness the power of transformed lives.

Our love for one another shows the world our unity with the Father, and also shows them that community requires unity—a oneness about the purposes of life. Jesus prayed to the Father, *"I pray that they may all be one. Father! May they be in us, just as you are in me and I am in you. May they be one, so that the world will believe that you sent me. I gave them the same glory you gave me, so that they may be one, just as you and I are one: I in them and you in me, so that they may be completely one, in order that the world may know that you sent me and that you love them as you love me"* (John 17:21-23).

Jesus says when we serve others, we serve him: *"I was hungry and you fed me, thirsty and you gave me a drink; I was a stranger and you received me in your homes, naked and you clothed me; I was sick and you took care of me, in prison and you visited me"* (Matthew 25:35).

But Jesus says it works the other way as well. Whenever someone helps us in our service to Jesus, they will be blessed with the same blessing we receive. So, Bonhoeffer notes, the "least" of us—the least experienced disciple, the youngest in faith—can help the most powerful of prophets and receive a share in that prophet's blessing.

This interconnectedness is a reflection of God's passion for oneness. We are one with Jesus in that our agenda submits to his; we show our oneness by obeying his commands. Jesus is one with the Father because he submits to the Father—and because we are submitted to Jesus, we also are one with the Father.

The call of Jesus is a call to love the Father so dearly that our hearts beat as one with his. We're compelled by the love of Jesus and because there are others following Jesus, who are also compelled by his love, we begin to move in unity with one heart and one mind, a body of Christ pursing the heart of the father together.

The apostle Paul uses the analogy of the body to teach us to develop this *healthy* dependence on each other within our connection to Jesus, *within the realm of costly grace.*

If you're a hand in the body of Christ, clearly you have an important role, but you won't be able to handle all the things God planned for you if you're not connected to the arm, the shoulder, and the head. We become dependent while we remain unique.

That some of us are thumbs, and others eyes, and others legs is proof that God designed us to live life together. We were never meant to journey with Jesus alone. As we each move closer to Jesus, it is only natural that we move closer to each other. Our shared connection with Jesus commands a higher standard than just getting along. He calls us to support and encourage *one another*, so even *the least of these* contributes to the whole, as we do ministry and mission together.

## BECOMING OTHER-CENTERED

Our journey with Jesus is designed to sever our ties to self-centeredness so that we will put the needs of others before our own: "None of you should be looking out for your own interests, but for the interests of others" (1 Corinthians 10:24).

It is the cycle of grace—Jesus empties himself to leave heaven in order to fill us with his Spirit and that enables us to empty ourselves for others so they will be drawn to Jesus. Jesus not only models self-sacrifice; he enables us to place the interests and concerns of others as the greater priority over our own.

In this way, we carry our unseen and eternal fellowship with Jesus—our oneness with God—into the nasty now-and-now of life here on earth that is seen yet temporary (Matthew 18:19–20). We're able to say, "We are from God, and we come with the same attitude of Jesus, not using the Spirit for our own interest, but emptying ourselves in sacrificial service to you" (paraphrase of 1 John 4:6; Philippians 2:5–7).

"Thus the disciples are bidden lastly to think, not about their own way, their own sufferings and their own reward, but of the goal of their labours, which is the salvation of the Church," says Bonhoeffer.

### The Cost of Discipleship—

Our journey with Jesus is designed to sever our ties to self-centeredness so that we will put the needs of others before our own.

### Fallen Thinking—

- I can live out the Christian faith without the help of Jesus and other believers.
- There are times when Jesus leaves me and I have to do life on my own.
- I can take care of all my own needs before I can take care of others.

### Kingdom Thinking—

- God's plan for my life is to partner with him for the redemption of the world.
- I will live today as the representation of Christ to those I encounter.
- "Love from the center of who you are; don't fake it. Run for dear life from evil; hold on for dear life to good" (Romans 12:9 MSG).

### Your Choice?

If Jesus is looking out for your interests, you are free to look out for the interests of others. It is in giving to them that you receive from Jesus—he gives to you so you can give to others. Will you join the flow of Jesus' giving?

# 27

## JESUS: YESTERDAY, TODAY, AND TOMORROW

*"If Christ is the living Lord of my life, my Christ is present."*
DIETRICH BONHOEFFER

*Jesus Christ is the same yesterday, today, and forever.*
HEBREWS 13:8

When Jesus called the disciples to follow, he stood physically before them; then, they spent nearly three years by his side. Bonhoeffer wonders if this gave the disciples an advantage over us? Did this make their discipleship different from our own?

Absolutely not! Jesus is the same yesterday, today, and tomorrow. There is only one Jesus. There isn't a Jesus who lived in Palestine and a Jesus who sits at the Father's right hand and a Jesus we invite into our hearts. *"There is one body and one Spirit, just as there is one hope to which God has called you," says the apostle Paul. "There is one Lord, one faith, one baptism; there is one God and Father of all people, who is Lord of all, works through all, and is in all"* (Ephesians 4:4-6).

The same Jesus who called the disciples to follow him is the same Jesus who calls you to follow him today.

And that means Jesus is alive; he is not some ancient teacher whose code can be applied to life today. He calls us to an intimate relationship where he inhabits our lives. Our call is not to a religion, certainly not to rituals, and in no way to meager "niceness."

Yet, we often speak as if he is dead. *What would Jesus have me do?* Well, why not just ask him?

We are like a child who keeps asking everyone, "What do you think my Father wants me to do?" *Why not go ask your father. Talk to him.*

We ask the question, "What would Jesus do?" and that actually suggests we have to figure out the answer on our own. It perpetuates the mythology that we are independent of Jesus or that we are forced into moral speculations when, in truth, we have the mind of Christ active and accessible within us. Otherwise, we are in the danger of becoming independent of Jesus. *I think this is what Jesus would do, so I will do it.*

So shouldn't the question be, "Jesus, what do you want me to do?" (JWDYWMTD) How else would you speak to a living person?

Can you see the difference?

"I think this is what Jesus would do, so I will do it."

"Jesus, I think this is what you want me to do, so I will do it."

## JESUS IS THE WORD

Jesus is the Word of God in the flesh. God's Word is dynamic and alive and, when we open the Bible, we are not merely referencing a moral code; we are interacting with the mind and heart of God. Jesus is the incarnation of God's Word come to us in the flesh. In him we see "the glory of the One and Only, who came from the Father, full of grace and truth" (John 1:14 NIV).

We see the testimony of Jesus and we have the same choice as the original disciples to decide if what he says is true. Bonheoffer notes, "Discipleship never consists in this or that specific action: it is always a decision, either for or against Jesus Christ. Hence our situation is not a whit less clear than that of the disciple or the publican in the gospel. When Jesus called his first disciples, they obeyed and followed him because they recognized him as the Christ."

We, too, must recognize him as Christ or else, like the Pharisees, we will study the Scriptures yet never understand the way into the kingdom of heaven (John 5:39-40).

And if we are confused, then Jesus calls us to concentrate on what we know—that he is the Messiah sent from God. We need only respond to him in obedience and he will light the path for us, providing the answers that we need as we need them. Otherwise, all our questions, all our systems for explaining God and Jesus, will distract us from the simple truth that in believing, we are able to obey—and when we obey, we are better able to believe.

## JESUS WITH THE HOLY SPIRIT

The Holy Spirit's presence in our lives is testimony to the truth that Jesus is alive and that his promises will be fulfilled. On the night before he died, Jesus said, "It's better for you that I leave. If I don't leave, the Friend won't come. But if I go, I'll send him to you. When he comes, he'll expose the error of the godless world's view of sin, righteousness, and judgment: He'll show them that their refusal to believe in me is their basic sin; that righteousness comes from above" (John 16:7-10 MSG).

In this way, the apostle Paul says, Christ lives in you "as you open the door and invite him in" (Ephesians 3:17 MSG).

"The scriptures do not present us with a series of Christian types to be imitated according to choice," says Bonhoeffer. "They preach to us in every situation the one Jesus Christ. To him alone must I listen. He is everywhere one and the same."

Jesus knows every step of the journey into the kingdom of heaven and he understands the blessings and dangers ahead. He never intended for you to figure out the steps of your journey without him. You don't have to know the reason for everything, and there's no requirement that you figure it all out before you start the journey. Jesus calls you to trust and obey. You're called to trust and obey, for there's no other way.

And Jesus, who is the same yesterday, today, and tomorrow, intercedes for you.

He prayed for you yesterday: "My prayer is not for them alone. I pray also for those who will believe in me through their message" (John 17:20 NIV).

He prays for you today: "Therefore he is able to save completely those who come to God through him, because he always lives to intercede for them" (Hebrews 7:25 NIV).

He prays for your tomorrow: "Father! You have given them to me, and I want them to be with me where I am, so that they may see my glory, the glory you gave me; for you loved me before the world was made" (John 17:24).

# 28

## JESUS AND THE SUFFERING SAINTS

*"Only Jesus Christ, who bids us follow him, knows the journey's end. But we do know that it will be a road of boundless mercy."*
DIETRICH BONHOEFFER.

*Jesus answered, "What God wants you to do is to believe in the one he sent."*
JOHN 6:29

One day the people couldn't find Jesus, so they went looking for him. When they found him, he was all the way on the other side of the Sea of Galilee, completely opposite from where they originally thought he would be (John 6:22-70).

"How long have you been here?" they asked.

Jesus didn't answer their specific question; instead, he spoke the truth in love, telling them that the only reason they followed him was because he'd given them free bread.

"You worked hard trying to find me, so you could get more bread," he said, in a sense. "Why work so hard for something that's so temporary? Put your efforts into things eternal."

The people asked, "What can we do in order to do what God wants us to do?"

Jesus answered, "What God wants you to do is to believe in the one he sent" (based on John 6:28-29).

Their search for Jesus had brought them to the opposite side of the lake from where they thought he would be and now he wanted them to start thinking opposite of their human nature, to stop thinking like mere mortals and start listening for the thoughts of God. He wanted them to enter into kingdom thinking and abandon their fallen thinking.

Jesus calls us to the same thing today. He wants us to enter into kingdom thinking and abandon our fallen thinking. We seek Jesus, thinking we know where we will find him—in religious traditions, in burdensome rules, in good behavior, in pious posturing; in feel-good fantasies that lead to cheap grace.

We ask, "What can we do in order to do what God wants us to do?" And Jesus says it's not about trying harder, but trusting more. What God wants you to do is obediently believe in the one he sent. Seek him and his righteousness and everything else will be provided.

Again, Jesus pushes to make a choice: Will we keep trying to find that one thing we must do, or will we simply trust Jesus and believe what he says?

He calls us to rest in him, trusting him to fulfill his promises. Instead of exhausting ourselves trying to please God, Jesus says we will please God when we put our efforts into believing the One sent by God, Jesus, the Father's own Son. We're to make every effort to enter the rest of God, not to earn the favor of God (Hebrews 4:1-14). This is the Sabbath rest of "Be still, and know that I am God," resting in the safety and security of his Word (Psalm 46:10 NIV).

Instead of trying harder, Jesus tells us to trust more.

Back in the day when God gave Moses the commandments, he said, in a sense, "This is what I'm like; these commandments reflect my holiness and my loving nature. If the people will keep these commandments, I will be their God and they will be my people."

But, then, God told Moses to hurry down the mountain. "They have already left the way that I commanded them to follow. They have made a bull-calf out of melted gold . . . . They are saying that this is their god, who led them out of Egypt." And he added, "I know how stubborn these people are" (Exodus 32:8, 9).

So Moses hurried down the mountain with "the two stone tablets on which God himself had written the commandments" (Exodus 31:18). But when Moses got close enough to the camp to see just how out of control the people were (that their worship feast had turned into an orgy of drinking and sex), he became angry and smashed the stone tablets at the foot of the mountain (based on Exodus 32:6; 32:19).

Right then the people would have been wise to say, "Yahweh, we can't follow your commandments. We can't meet your standards. Only you are capable of such goodness."

But they didn't.

When Moses went back up the mountain for a second set of commandments, God said, "I, the Lord, am a God who is full of compassion and pity, who is not easily angered and who shows great love and faithfulness" (Exodus 34:6).

Again, the people would have been wise to call upon God's compassion and mercy and to fall upon his grace. In fact, God wanted them to rest in his promises, to trust in his character (Hebrews 4:1-14). But these were a stubborn people and so they said, "Okay, we'll do it. We'll keep the commandments. We'll keep all the rules."

The Old Testament is a history of the fact that they couldn't do it.

In the Old Testament, they served God by trying to keep the Law and offering sacrifices—and, then, periodically and ritualistically asking for their sins to be forgiven.

How do we try to serve God? By trying to keep the Law and offering sacrifices—those things we do to try to make up for the things we've done wrong—and then asking for forgiveness because we've failed. We can't do it.

But that's not the way it is supposed to work. Even the Old Testament prophets knew God didn't want the blood of bulls and goats. He wanted a contrite heart, a heart submitted and obedient to him (Psalm 51).

The thing is, God knew we couldn't do it either. The apostle Paul told the Galatians, "The obvious impossibility of carrying out such a moral program should make it plain that no one can sustain a relationship with God that way. The person who lives in right relationship with God does it by embracing what God arranges for him. Doing things for God is the opposite of entering into what God does for you. Habakkuk had it right: 'The person who believes God, is set right by God—and that's the real life'" (Galatians 3:11 MSG).

Paul added, "Rule-keeping does not naturally evolve into living by faith, but only perpetuates itself in more and more rule-keeping . . . Christ redeemed us from that self-defeating, cursed life by absorbing it completely into himself" (Galatians 3:12a, 13a MSG).

God knew the only way we could return to intimacy with him was by writing the commandments into our hearts and not on tablets of stone (2 Corinthians 3:3). And he did this in his own hand, giving us his own Son, an incarnation of his Word, who was "full of grace and truth" (John 1:14).

In Jesus, the Father's only Son, the fullness of divine nature lives and, through Christ, we have "been given full life in union with him" (Colossians 2:9-10a). In other words, we are complete in Christ. At the moment of conversion, we are given everything we need to succeed at the abundant life, everything we need to live a life of extraordinary quality, one that carries significance beyond ourselves.

The character of Christ is already at work in us; the mind of Christ is already available to us. We are "more than conquerors through him who loved us" (Romans 8:37 NIV). We now "come from God and belong to God" and "the Spirit in [us] is far stronger than anything in the world" (1 John 4:4 MSG).

There is nothing we can do to add to what God has already done. Nothing.

Our job is to trust and rest in the truth that our safety and security is in Jesus. The full and complete life of Christ that is already in us will emerge, not because we try harder, but because we obediently trust the Word of God.

"My counsel for you is simple and straightforward: Just go ahead with what you've been given," says Paul. "You received Christ Jesus, the Master; now live him. You're deeply rooted in him. You're well constructed upon him. You know your way around the faith. Now do what you've been taught. School's out; quit studying the subject and start living it! And let your living spill over into thanksgiving" (Colossians 2:6-7 MSG).

Jesus calls us to do this today, to not be stubborn like the people at Mt. Sinai, but to obediently enter the rest of God by stepping into his costly grace (Hebrews 4:7).

To echo Oswald Chambers, Jesus calls us to follow him into the kingdom of heaven, and when we hesitate, he asks, "Do you not want to be a saint, or do you not believe God can make you one?"[15]

Because you already are one and have been since the life of Christ entered your heart. "It is he who made us capable of serving the new covenant, which consists not of a written law but of the Spirit. The written law brings death, but the Spirit gives life" (2 Corinthians 3:6).

We trust that Jesus has done the work required for us to boldly approach the throne of God and we rest faithfully in the truth that we can now enter the kingdom of heaven under his banner of righteousness. We believe we are holy, just as our heavenly Father is holy, because Jesus is the one who makes us holy (1 Peter 1:16).

It was their refusal to believe this that brought on Paul's rebuke of the Galatians: "Tell me this one thing: did you receive God's Spirit by doing what the Law requires or by hearing the gospel and believing it? How can you be so foolish! You began by God's Spirit; do you now want to finish by your own power?" (Galatians 3:2-3).

We begin the journey into the kingdom upon our completion in Christ—and that is at the moment of salvation. The journey makes us aware of the One who lives in us and Jesus uses the journey to teach us how to grow-up in Christ, so that who we are on the outside matches the life of Christ that flows through our inside,

May you know joy in the journey and may you know with radiant certainty that Jesus, the Word of God, fulfills every one of his promises. He obediently trusted the Father so that you could enter the kingdom of heaven; may you obediently trust Jesus to get you through the narrow gate, where the Father and all of heaven will celebrate your return home (Luke 15:32).

# ENDNOTES

1   Eberhard Bethge, *Dietrich Bonhoeffer: A Biography,* revised edition (Minneapolis: Augsburg Fortress, 2000).

2   This short section is based on Paul Carlisle and Jon Walker, "How Grace Can Transform You and Your Church," *Rick Warren's Ministry Toolbox*, Issue 98, 04-16-2003. Copyright Paul Carlisle and Jon Walker. All rights reserved. Used by permission.

3   July 2, Oswald Chambers, *My Utmost for His Highest*, version found in WORDsearch 8, 2020 –Preaching Edition, Build 8.0.2.71.

4   June 29, Oswald Chambers, *My Utmost for His Highest*.

5   Jim Elliot's Journal, October 28, 1949.

6   Quoted in Rick Warren, *The Purpose Driven Church* (Zondervan, 1995), 372.

7   April 29, Oswald Chambers, *My Utmost for His Highest*.

8   See the story of Rahab in Joshua 2:1-14; Hebrews 11:31.

9   Matthew 5:42 in *The MacArthur New Testament Commentary, Matthew 1-7* (Chicago: Moody Bible Institute, 1985). As found in Database © 2008 WORDsearch Corp.

10  Peter Lord was the pastor of Park Avenue Baptist Church in Titusville, Florida for thirty years and is the author of the "2959 Plan," a plan for focused prayer. You can learn more about his ministry at http://peterlord.net/.

11  November 23, Oswald Chambers, *My Utmost for His Highest*.

12  Matthew 7:6 in *MacArthur New Testament Commentary*.

13  Matthew 7:24-27 in ibid.

14  Henry Blackaby and Claude King, *Experiencing God: Knowing and Doing the Will of God*, revised edition (Nashville: Broadman & Holman , 2008).

15  June 12, Oswald Chambers, *My Utmost for His Highest*.